Julian of Norwich

Selected Books in the
SkyLight Illuminations Series

Julian of Norwich

Selections from
Revelations of Divine Love—
Annotated & Explained

Annotation by Mary C. Earle

Foreword by Roberta C. Bondi

Walking Together, Finding the Way ®

SKYLIGHT PATHS®
PUBLISHING
Woodstock, Vermont

Julian of Norwich:
Selections from Revelations of Divine Love—*Annotated & Explained*

2013 Quality Paperback Edition, First Printing
Introduction and annotation © 2013 by Mary C. Earle
Foreword © 2013 by Roberta C. Bondi

Library of Congress Cataloging-in-Publication Data
Earle, Mary C.
Julian of Norwich : selections from Revelations of divine love : annotated & explained / Mary C. Earle ; foreword by Roberta Bondi. — Quality paperback edition.
      pages cm
Includes bibliographical references.
ISBN 978-1-59473-513-4
1. Julian, of Norwich, 1343- Revelations of divine love. 2. Mysticism—Catholic Church. 3. Mysticism—England—History—Middle Ages, 600-1500. I. Julian, of Norwich, 1343- Revelations of divine love. Selections. English. II. Title.
BV5095.J84E27 2013
242—dc23
                                                    2013037112

10   9   8   7   6   5   4   3   2   1
Manufactured in the United States of America
Cover Design: Walter C. Bumford III, Stockton, Massachusetts
Cover Art: Elizabeth Hinton-Simoneau © Julian Centre, www.friendsofjulian.org.uk

SkyLight Paths, "Walking Together, Finding the Way" and colophon are trademarks of LongHill Partners, Inc., registered in the U.S. Patent and Trademark Office.

Walking Together, Finding the Way®
Published by SkyLight Paths Publishing
A Division of LongHill Partners, Inc.
Sunset Farm Offices, Route 4, P.O. Box 237
Woodstock, VT 05091
Tel: (802) 457-4000   Fax: (802) 457-4004
www.skylightpaths.com

For Doug,
who knows that
"love is oure lordes mening"

Contents ☐

Foreword ☐

Roberta C. Bondi

I first encountered the writings of Julian of Norwich in 1979 when a friend of mine sent me a copy of the Short Text of Julian's *Revelations of Divine Love*. I knew nothing about Julian at the time; I hadn't heard of her in seminary church history courses and I had never heard her mentioned afterward. Nevertheless, here she was, a fourteenth-century English woman who had had visions, who had written about them (and, as I learned, was the first woman to write a piece of literature in English), and whose work, somehow or another, had been preserved for the future. Considering that it was 1979 and I had just been appointed to the first tenure-track position a woman had ever held, the very existence of Julian was a revelation in itself. As a woman in such a place as I was, I needed all the moral support I could get.

Unfortunately, at that point, I was not able to benefit much from her. I had had enough exposure to hellfire-and-brimstone Christianity growing up that, whatever I believed in my head at that point, I simply could not believe in my bones that her central convictions about God's absolute love for human beings as well as God's total lack of judgment of us could be true. Yes, of course, God loved me, but deep inside in some inaccessible childhood place, I knew I was a sinner. Human beings were sinners and God's predictable, dependable rage over everyone's sin was simply inescapable. When it came to God, I was doomed, all of us were doomed.

Then, there was the whole issue of being female in the difficult-for-women culture in which I had grown up and begun to teach: in my first university job, I once was present at a conversation where an important scholar in my department was asked what he thought of a woman teaching at the undergraduate and graduate levels. "I think it is fine," he responded, "so long as she gets her housework done and her husband gives her permission." To this day, I believe as a woman I was so invisible to him that he was not even aware of my presence.

Though I would have denied it before I read her, that I did believe these horrific things in my bones is what I first learned from Julian. I learned it by reading her, immediately falling into a depression, and then having to figure out where my depression had come from. After much pondering, I recognized that I wanted to believe her with my whole heart. I saw very well how I would be able to be myself, a human being and a woman, with God in a world where I could belong, where all things were created, sustained, and completed in God's absolute love. With my whole heart, I yearned for Julian's words to be true, but I was as far from being able to believe them as sugar is from salt, and so I grieved and I grieved.

I am not sure at what point I found the Long Text of her *Revelations* in which, many years later after bringing forth the Short Text, she filled out, corrected, and explained what she had come more fully to understand about God and humans, about the Trinity, about the identity of Jesus, about God's love for all that God has created, about God's motherhood, about the part of each of us that never consents to sin and is always kept safe and whole in God, about the inevitable but blameless suffering that mortality entails in all of us, and above all, about God's promise that at the end of all things, all, absolutely everything, will be well, brought to completion in God's love exactly as God intended it from the beginning, and we ourselves will see that it is so.

By the time I met her again, I had spent years with the desert fathers and mothers of the ancient monastic tradition. They, out of their infinite grace, mercy, and love, had already convinced me of the total lack of judgment that went with the kind of love of God into which they sought to grow. By their own kindness, they had nearly freed me from a sense that God held me always under judgment and always found me lacking.

At last the time came when I could hear and begin to understand much of the rest of the good news Jesus from the cross had shared with Julian, and which he had insisted he gave to her not just for her in her own time, but also for all her fellow Christians, right up until the present.

And how very many of Julian's fellow Christians in our own time particularly need this news! On the one hand, the varieties of Christianity that still link the wrath of God to the love of God are growing. It hasn't been very long, after all, since I passed a huge billboard along a big highway in a major American city that informed drivers and passengers: "God loves you," it said, "turn and burn." On the other hand, people of all ages are now leaving the churches and abandoning Christianity altogether because, I believe, they don't realize that Christians have any other way to know God except in these poisonous terms.

How many women still need what Julian has to say about the universality of the motherhood of God! How many women are still told that women have no place in ordained ministry, or are still subjected to the whole idea of male "headship" of the family! How many working women supporting families on their own are still—as I was at the beginning of my career—accused one way or another of taking jobs from men, who need them to support their families! Julian's way of speaking of the motherhood of God affirms the dignity of our femaleness in all its aspects, including the physical ones.

Some of what is most important for us to hear, however, is hard to get to. The Long Text of Julian, the one we really need, however, is difficult to follow unless the reader is prepared to read it over and over again. No one could miss Julian's overriding message of the absolute, unconditional, unqualified love "the Blessed Trinity" has for all of us, indeed, for all that God has made. For many of us who have been wounded by religion, this is enough. For those of us like I was back in 1979, and like Julian herself, obviously, the assertion of God's love is not enough. In the

Long Text of the *Revelations* Jesus tells Julian over and over that God is not concerned with human sin, and Julian politely but insistently tells Jesus that she would like to believe him, but he needs to convince her. It is not until she is given the revelation of the lord and servant is she able to see this as true. As with Julian herself, assertions are not enough for us; we, too, need the arguments.

But in spite of the simplicity of her main theme of God's love for us, Julian is a very complex thinker and experiencer of God who is the Trinity, and the arguments are not always easy to understand. What Mary Earle has done for her readers in this little book is to cut pathways through Julian. By providing excerpts from the text arranged by topics, and then by further providing short commentaries on these excerpts, the new, and not so new, reader of Julian can, at last, find ways into her depths, where we can truly meet God, the world, each other, and ourselves in the delightful fullness of God's love for us.

Acknowledgments ☐

I owe a debt of gratitude to Emily Wichland for inviting me to author this book on Julian of Norwich. I have long loved this material, and the privilege of being immersed in Julian's text and the work of various scholars has been a fine and lovely gift. Nancy Fitzgerald kindly saw the possibility of offering my name to SkyLight Paths. Cynthia Shattuck's editorial skill has been of immense help. I am grateful to Roberta C. Bondi for offering the foreword; her scholarship and her example have shaped my own life and teaching. Fr. Ronald Rolheiser, president of Oblate School of Theology in San Antonio, and Rose Marden, dean for continuing education, have given me opportunities to present this material over the past couple of years in continuing education settings. My students at the Seminary of the Southwest in Austin embraced Julian's writings in the elective courses that I offered; their insights and questions have traveled with me over the years. Dr. Madeline Sutherland-Meier of the University of Texas at Austin, who supported the doctoral work that I never finished, offered steady and firm encouragement for my love of medieval women's writings. Our conversations, now almost twenty years ago, oriented my years of study and confirmed the insights that women bring to texts written by women.

Lastly, my son, Jason, and husband, Doug, have encouraged me along the way with this particular endeavor. Their interest and support mean more than I can say.

Introduction ☐

You've just come home from the hospital. Or the divorce papers have just been signed. Or perhaps there's been a death in the family. Or your beloved cat or dog has had to be put down. Then the mail arrives. You open an envelope and see a card from a friend. On the front, the card bears this line: "All Shall Be Well." The line is attributed to "Julian of Norwich, fourteenth century."

What in the world does this mean, "All shall be well"? And how are you to construe it in the midst of whatever personal loss, suffering, or bereavement has occasioned the sender's choice of this card?

For many, the rich text from which "all shall be well" has been extracted is unknown and unremarked. The author, known to us simply as Julian of Norwich, is also probably an unknown. Yet if we do a Google search of the phrase "all shall be well," we rapidly discover that the phrase has been used in literature, poetry, music, and greeting cards. Even Pete Townshend, of the rock band The Who, has composed a song using Julian's words as a refrain.

My own journey with Julian's writings began in 1977 when I was raising my two young sons, one of them newborn. I found myself drawn to the Gospel of John and then to the fourteenth-century English mystics, especially Julian of Norwich and the anonymous author of *The Cloud of Unknowing.* At the time, I was teaching Spanish at a local university, raising my boys, enjoying domestic life with my husband, Doug, and being drawn steadily toward what I came to know as contemplative prayer. Another friend and mother of four, Suzanne Guthrie, pointed me toward Julian's *Revelations of Divine Love*. While I had some training in literary theory and analysis, I had never read anything like Julian's text. I was both completely confounded and magnetically drawn to her insights. It was a process of unknowing and discovering, of finding anew the depth and the breadth of my Christian faith tradition and of the spiritual life.

My own life at the time was a balance of the domestic and the professional. I was preparing lesson plans for teaching while nursing a baby, bathing those two sons, preparing their meals, and continually (as most mothers do) handling the various bodily fluids coming forth from such young bodies. I had no real use for theology that was a complete abstraction. A life-long Episcopalian, I had been nurtured by *The Book of Common Prayer* and the normative observance of the seasons of the church year (Advent, Christmas, Epiphany, Lent, Easter, Pentecost, ordinary time). At the same time, I had received no instruction about contemplative prayer, which was oddly taking hold within me in the midst of the rounds of washing clothes, preparing food, dealing with my own changing body, tending to the physical needs of two dear little boys, and gardening.

It was Julian who offered me needed counsel. She told me that God is the foundation of prayer (LT 41, p. 99).[1] She invited me to see that God is to us as clothing—close and familiar. She even blessed the daily round of diaper changing, remarking that God has so well designed the body that it "opens daily like a purse." She gave me this prayer: "God of your goodness, give me yourself; you are enough for me" (LT 5, p. 48). Astonishingly, at a time in the late 1970s when I was barely aware of the debates around inclusive language, patriarchal influences, and the need for recovering feminine imagery for God, Julian was telling me that God is our mother! This language, in the midst of my own intense and personal practice of being a mother, resonated with me fully, body and soul, even though I did not completely understand the theological implications of her language. Here was a companion in the way of prayer, someone whose words and insights began to form my own practice and perspective when I was twenty-nine years old.

Several years later, when I enrolled as a seminary student and began wrestling with the possibility of being ordained a priest in the Episcopal Church, I read Julian again. This time, while carrying the almost visceral experience of her text forward, I was also stopped in my tracks by her religious imagination. Julian's emphasis on seeing, beholding, and insight spoke deeply. Her words are birthed from images. As she reflects over many years, those sixteen *shewings* (the Middle English word that she uses, meaning both "revelation" and "exposure," or "showing forth") offer up further insight. Her experience and her prayer lead her to see new layers of meaning and connection. The original vision, wedded to meaning and interpretation, continues to shape and generate her theology as she reflects and prays for some twenty years. Her text is structured around the sequence of these sixteen visions. As a result, from time to time, you will find her referring to a particular showing, referencing something that she has already mentioned.

In discovering this aspect of Julian's text, I found an antidote to the deep-seated habit of instant interpretation that so infects our culture. As pervasive as that habit was at the time I was in seminary in the 1980s, it is now epidemic. Instant news appears to lead to instant insight, which is surely a delusion. That practice might work in the newsroom, but it never works in the life of prayer. As the poet T. S. Eliot wrote in "The Dry Salvages," "We had the experience but we missed the meaning."[2]

Compare this to Julian, who took some twenty years to reflect, ponder, and write about the shewings given to her in 1373. She waited patiently for the meaning to be made known. She embodied the stance of intellectual and spiritual humility offered in the Wisdom of Solomon: "The beginning of wisdom is the most sincere desire for instruction" (Wisdom 7:17). Julian's natural humility—the humility that knows how much one can never fully know and recognizes the limits of finite human beings in discerning divine truth and love—shines through the text. Yet Julian is never servile, nor is she puffed up. She has the temerity to ask direct questions of God about what the visions mean and how she is to perceive the truth within. Faithfully and patiently, she devotes herself to the task of knitting together word and image, feeling and insight. The result is a text that demands close reading and that resembles intricate knitting, finely and skillfully crafted. This is a work whose patient creation invites patient reading. It is also a text that may seem repetitive, when in fact different insights are mutually illuminating. The text is almost a Celtic knot, one of those designs in which the lines form a harmonious whole, yet continually intersect and reconnect with one another.

Since those initial encounters with *Revelations of Divine Love*, I have read the text many times; taught it in parish, retreat, and seminary settings; used it as guidance for offering spiritual direction; and found needed counsel and wisdom when in the midst of personal loss and disorientation. In this volume, I hope to offer the reader, particularly those who are not well acquainted with Julian's writings, an opportunity to discover the treasure of this text. As is the case with all of the volumes in the SkyLight Illuminations series, this book is intended for the general reader, though it may also be of use to those who have some familiarity with *Revelations of Divine Love*. Julian represents the genre of vernacular mysticism, works that are written in the spoken language of their day rather than in Latin or Greek. Because she intends the text for her *evenchristen* (fellow laywomen and -men), her tone is conversational. She is writing in the language of the people she knows and to whom she listens; her words are shaped by her own daily speaking and the ordinary exchanges with other citizens of Norwich. For that reason I have used the translation done by Elizabeth Spearing, published by Penguin Books in 1998, recommended to me as a translation that happily reflects this conversational rhythm and tone of her Middle English.

It is important to remember that Julian's style, while conversational, also reflects her times. She uses traditional doctrinal language and is at pains to make sure that her terms are acceptable to the church. That said, the terms that we may hear as impersonal and doctrinal, such as her language about the Trinity, are to her familiar and deeply personal.

Who Was Julian of Norwich?

The author Sheila Upjohn, in her book *In Search of Julian of Norwich,* notes that trying to discover the true identity of Julian requires a lot of detective work.[3] The manuscript itself remained hidden for some time. In it the woman known as Julian tells us that she was given these shewings: "These revelations were shown to a simple, uneducated creature in the year of our Lord 1373, on the eighth day of May" (LT 2, p. 42). A contemporary of Geoffrey Chaucer, Julian is the first woman author known to write in English. She tells us that she suddenly became so ill that a priest was sent for. As he held a crucifix before her eyes, Julian suddenly *saw* the bleeding Jesus before her, and heard him speak to her. Her manuscript records what she saw, what she heard, and what she came to understand as she reflected on the experience.

Julian wrote two versions of her intense visionary experience. The first, known as the Short Text, was probably composed within a short period after she recovered from her illness. The second, known as the Long Text, is the fruit of some twenty years of pondering, reflecting, waiting, self-questioning, and discerning. The Long Text differs from the shorter by including the parable of the lord and the servant as well as Julian's insight into God as our mother. This is the text I have chosen to use and excerpt for this commentary (abbreviated as "LT" throughout).

Julian's manuscript does not tell us her life story. At its conclusion she disappears, in a way, despite the fact that the experience is intensely personal. Her ongoing conversation with Jesus as he is dying draws her into the text, and into our imaginations. Yet we have very little to go on with regard to her personal life.

Over the years, some scholars have speculated that she was a Benedictine nun because of the level of learning exhibited by her writing. Others have thought that she might have been a widow who became an anchorite—an enclosed solitary recluse—when she had the visions. Many have said that we cannot truly know the name of the author because she probably took it from the parish church of St. Julian's. Fr. John-Julian, OJN, has carefully examined fourteenth-century wills and other testimonial documents. He postulates that she may have been a wealthy laywoman, Julian Erpingham, who was widowed twice and bore several children.[4] Sr. Benedicta Ward, SLG, maintains that there is nothing in the text itself that would indicate that Julian was a nun—no references to liturgical hours or the cloistered life. Instead, she proposes that the text is written by a woman who had experienced the death of a child (or children) during the Black Death of the late 1340s.[5] Julian's language for God as "Mother," in Sr. Benedicta's opinion, may come from her wrenching experience of the death of a child.

We know that Julian was visited in 1413 by Margery Kempe, another English laywoman who wrote her spiritual autobiography.[6] Given that Julian tells us that she was thirty years old at the time that she fell gravely ill and was gifted with the vision in 1373, it appears that she lived a long life. But the bottom line is that we can't fully know who Julian was, nor can we glean complete details of her life. It seems that she wanted it that way. In her text, Julian makes clear that she hopes that the reader will pay attention not to her but to the teaching that she hands on—teaching that she has received from her visions and then refined by years of prayer and reflection.

Julian's Context: The Fourteenth Century

Julian lived at a time of vast social and political upheaval, incessant wars, and sweeping epidemics. Norwich, with a population of around 25,000 by 1330[7] and perhaps the second largest town in England during Julian's lifetime, was struck viciously by the plague known as the Black Death.

At its peak in the late 1340s in England, it killed approximately three-fourths of the population of Norwich. A young girl at this time, Julian was certainly affected in untold ways by this devastation. When the plague returned she was about nineteen, so it is within the realm of possibility that she was married with a child. Although we cannot know for sure, her life must have been indelibly changed by the deaths of those nearest and dearest to her.

In a social and cultural context so saturated with suffering and death, it is no wonder that many believers interpreted these as clear signs of God's anger with humanity. (Certainly we still see vestiges of this way of interpreting events; remember the voices of those who spoke of Hurricane Katrina as being a divine judgment upon New Orleans, the visitation of an angry god.) The underlying theology draws on a medieval doctrine known as substitutionary atonement, elucidated by Anselm of Canterbury in the eleventh century. The popular version of this theology held (as it still does today) that because of our many sins, we owe God a debt we can never repay—our burden of debt is so vast and we are finite. That is why Jesus, by dying on the cross, offers himself as a way of making retribution on our behalf: the Son offers himself as a sacrifice in order to satisfy the Father's wrath. It is easy to see how this theology in its crudest form evolved into a belief in an angry and vengeful God, visiting humanity with punishing events.

Thus in Julian's day popular devotional art often depicted horrific scenes of the Last Judgment, scenes in which souls were being cast into hell, tortured endlessly by devils. Laymen and -women of the fourteenth century would have constantly been wrestling with the "Why?" of suffering and the wrath of God. As any nurse, doctor, social worker, or clergy person knows, when someone receives a terminal diagnosis, or a sudden death occurs, or a natural disaster devastates a region, the first question that occurs is usually, "Why me? What did we do to deserve this? Why is God punishing me?" The context out of which Julian writes, although in some ways so remote from our own, is one full of universal questions and themes. Julian offers a transformational way of seeing and a deliverance from this kind of theological entrapment.

Julian tells us, again and again, in a variety of ways, that God is our friend, our mother and our father, as close to us as the clothing we wear. She employs homely imagery and language, the vocabulary of domesticity, to tell us her experience. At the same time, she demonstrates a degree of sophisticated theological language. Julian is firm and steady on these points:

- God is One.
- Everything is in God.
- God is in everything.
- God transcends and encloses all that is made.

She is also deeply trinitarian in her thinking, by which I mean that she speaks of the one God being revealed to be three persons held together by the bonds of love. Using the traditional language of Father, Son, and Holy Ghost (now we usually say "Holy Spirit"), she makes clear that from her own reflection and prayer, she knows the Trinity to be a communion of divine love; Father, Son, and Holy Spirit mutually dwell in each other in an infinite love. The communion of these three is so immeasurably profound that it *is* one. While we of the twenty-first century may think of the doctrine of the Trinity as a complex theological formula, Julian, as mystic and theologian, does not "think" the Trinity. She has encountered and been transformed by the single love that is known in uniquely personal relationship in prayer. In some ways, her trinitarian language is reminiscent of the Celtic prayers that speak of "the Three of my love."

Furthermore, because Jesus is fully human and fully divine, he fully represents all of humanity and all of divinity. Julian says clearly, "Where Jesus is spoken of, the Holy Trinity is to be understood" (LT 4, p. 46). So, when Julian has the vision of Jesus bleeding on the cross, she comes to know that Jesus is a shewing of divine love, a revelation of the Trinity.

God's infinite compassion is revealed to Julian, in her time of greatest physical weakness, when Jesus cheerfully says, "If I could suffer more, I would suffer more" (LT 22, p. 72).

In her experience of suffering, Julian starts from a different question. Instead of "Why me?" she begins with the vision of a tiny hazelnut held in the palm of one hand: "In this vision he also showed a little thing, the size of a hazelnut in the palm of my hand, and it was as round as a ball. I looked at it with my mind's eye and thought, 'What can this be?' And the answer came to me, 'It is all that is made'" (LT 5, p. 47). This starting point leads her to see reality from God's own perspective, or, at the very least, to consider the limitations of her own perspective. She is gripped by the littleness of all that is when seen in relationship to infinite love. As Jesus suffers on the cross, the whole of divine love is revealed. As scholar Roberta Bondi has remarked with regard to Julian's insights, "No one is doing anything to anybody in the crucifixion. This is love, divine love."[8]

Further, all of this insight is given to Julian as she beholds Jesus bleeding on the cross just as she herself seems to be in the midst of dying. Julian leads us to see that in Jesus's suffering and death, the divine love that made us and will not let us go accompanies us through every harrowing experience. God is always with us in every instant, present within each space and each time. Julian allows us to see that suffering is not God's punishment, but an inevitable aspect of life. If we live long enough, we will suffer. In the Passion of Jesus, God shews us that the divine life is entwined with every moment of our own despair and disorientation. As Bondi asks:

> If we look at our own suffering and death as somehow abnormal and blamable, how can we think of the crucifixion as anything other than a blood sacrifice made to satisfy God? How can we possibly see Jesus's death for what it was—as terrible, but also unavoidable in some form, given God's loving decision to enter fully into the Incarnation to share our mortal lot? How can we trust the love of God at all unless we *see* that love?[9]

Julian uses the word "sin" throughout her revelations, and it is important to know what she intends by that word. On the one hand, she clearly means that when we sin, we are living and behaving in ways that hurt ourselves and others. On the other, she understands that sin is caused by our spiritual blindness, our failure to see clearly, which is caused by our ignorance. The blindness is healed as we awaken from our ignorance and receive the divine love that has brought us into being.

No matter what our faith tradition, Julian's radical insistence that we know there is "no anger in God" (LT 13, p. 61) directs us all to look at ways in which we project our own bitterness, anger, and vengeance upon God. In a resolutely maternal way, she encourages us to grow up, to cast aside our immature and punitive images of God, and to be honest with ourselves about our own actions that have their roots in spiritual blindness.

As is the case with the mystical way, Julian's perception that everything is in God has moral implications. If all is in God—ourselves and our neighbors and all that is created—then all is inherently sacred. Julian's text is one that challenges us to recognize that *how* we see shapes *what* we see. If we behold one another as beings in whom the love that makes and sustains us dwells, and allow that to be our primary lens for perceiving reality, we have to ask ourselves the hard questions. We awaken to the fact that we are called to honor God's own life within all.

Medieval Women's Visionary Literature

From the first paragraphs of Julian's text it is clear that *Revelations of Divine Love* is visionary literature from the medieval English tradition. Already we know that we are encountering a world far different from our own. From a twenty-first-century viewpoint, the experience of religious visions tends to mark someone as mentally unstable. We might invoke leaders like Martin Luther King Jr. when we want to speak of political and social visions—but what if someone we know tells us that she has seen a vision of Jesus on the cross, speaking directly to her?

And yet that is what happened to Julian. Her text comes forth from the experience of beholding Jesus, bleeding copiously on the cross. That, in and of itself, might lead you the reader to put this book down and find a good novel. (Once, when I was teaching a seminar on *Revelations of Divine Love* to students at divinity school, one of them blurted out, "Am I the only person in this class who thinks Julian is totally nuts?")

In the medieval church, the religious imagination was held in much higher esteem. The culture of the church encouraged an openness to visions, even though these visions always needed to be tested for truth. A world of image, color, and pattern, the medieval church offered scriptural narratives through the sculptures adorning sanctuaries, through mystery plays, and through soaring stained glass depictions of Jesus's conception, birth, life, crucifixion, death, and resurrection. Because so many of the laity were illiterate, the church sought to teach through art.

Furthermore, as scholars such as Elizabeth Petroff have shown, devout medieval women were open to visions as direct engagements with God.[10] In an ecclesiastical world that prohibited formal education and a voice in the church, let alone women's ordination to priestly life, the invitation to a vowed celibate life offered a kind of freedom. As vehicles for inner transformation, their visions empowered such women to discover their own identity in God. As they learned from Scripture, the gift of visions had a prophetic dimension: "Visions were a socially sanctioned activity that freed a woman from conventional female roles by identifying her as a genuine religious figure. They brought her to the attention of others, giving her a public language she could use to teach and learn. Finally, visions allowed the medieval woman to be an artist, composing and refining her most profound experiences into a form that she could create and recreate for herself throughout her entire life."[11] The visions, always intensely personal, were also encounters intended to strengthen others.

Julian is clear from the very beginning that she is mindful of her status as a woman and that she hopes to benefit others through her writing:

> And what I say of myself, I am saying on behalf of all my fellow Christians, for I was taught in the spiritual showing of our Lord God that that is his purpose; and therefore I beg you all for God's sake and advise you for your own advantage that you stop paying attention to the poor being to whom this vision was shown, and eagerly and attentively and humbly contemplate God, who in his gracious love and eternal goodness wanted the vision to be generally known to comfort us all; for it is God's will that you should receive it with joy and pleasure as great as if Jesus had shown it to you all. (LT 8, p. 53)

Julian's visions are intrinsically powerful, in other words, because they are not hers. They are given to her so that she might hand them on to others.

Finally, in her theology of hope and steadfast love, Julian declares that God is our mother. During the medieval period, it was not unusual for monks and nuns to write about Jesus as a mother who feeds us with his own body, just as a mother feeds a baby with her breast milk. Julian takes this one step further. She focuses the work of divine grace in declaring Jesus (and therefore God) to be our mother. As we shall see in the texts that follow, Julian states that we come forth from God's own life, and we are made new by God in Jesus's Passion, rebirthed in joy through Jesus's self-offering. Motherhood, for Julian, is the primary way of articulating the Incarnation and redemption shown to her in Jesus on the cross.

Throughout her writings Julian offers the reader sound spiritual direction, for she expands our images for God and rejects any residual notions of God as an avenging, angry presence. She leads us to open our minds, our hearts, and our imaginations, so that we may receive the divine love that makes, sustains, and cares for us. When she hears the words "all shall be well," she receives them as words offering eternal hope from the One who is mother, father, friend, spouse, and love incarnate.

Julian of Norwich

1 Julian's visions began at the moment when, apparently near death, she beheld a crucifix brought by her priest. When the priest elevated the cross with its crucified body of Jesus, Julian began to receive her series of sixteen shewings—a Middle English word primarily meaning "revelation." New Testament accounts of Jesus's crucifixion tell of his being given a crown of thorns and mocked by the Roman cohort, who knelt before him saying, "Hail, King of the Jews!"

2 Julian's theology is distinctive in its insistence on the oneness of all, and she illustrates this again and again with reference to the Trinity. While referring to God as three—Father, Son, and Holy Ghost—she also has encountered the singleness of "making, loving, and caring" that is divine love.

3 In Jesus, God reveals that the divine and the human are intimately made for each other and can never be separated. God dwells in all of creation. If this were not the case, there would be no creation, no creatures, and no human beings, because all is brought forth from the inexhaustible love of God.

4 The showings were given to Julian when she appeared to be dying. In that time of letting go, she began her twenty-year journey of see-ing, knowing, reflecting, and writing. Her book is the fruit of a long process of allowing herself to be taught while also asking forthrightly in prayer for deeper understanding. The visions she receives become the point of departure for seeing that "in [Christ] all things hold together" (Colossians 1:17b).

1 □ The Visions

The first is of his precious crowning with thorns,[1] and by this was understood and specified the Trinity with the Incarnation[2] and unity between God and the soul of man,[3] with many fair showings of unending wisdom and teaching of love, on which all the showings that follow are founded and in which they are all united.[4]

LT 1, P. 41

5   Julian's self-description has been debated by many scholars. "Uned-ucated" seems to mean her lack of formal training in Latin and theol-ogy, although Julian did know the Bible and was clearly capable of theological reflection. She wrote in Middle English, the vernacular of her day, to communicate with her evenchristen, all of her sisters and brothers in the faith.

6   Julian's feast day is observed on May 8 in the Anglican calendar, though she has never been beatified or canonized by the Roman Cath-olic Church.

7   Note that these three requests involve suffering in various degrees. Julian asks to see clearly the suffering that Jesus endured on the cross, which was a devotional practice of her time, and also requests that she undergo an illness, as a means of knowing suffering from the inside out. While this focus on pain may appear strange to us, in the four-teenth century, surrounded as people were by death caused by plague, famine, and war, joining oneself to the suffering of Jesus was a way of compassionately participating in the pain of the world.

8   Julian possesses a highly vivid religious imagination. Here she prays to imagine what it was like to stand at the foot of the cross with Mary the mother of Jesus, Mary Magdalene, and other disciples who watched as Jesus died. She seeks a prayerful awareness of the sorrow of being with another in pain, without the power to change, or to heal, or to transform.

9   Julian may have known first-hand the experience of watching help-lessly over the dying, as Jesus's friends did. We know that Norwich had been ravaged by the plague, so she may have stood at the bed-side of dying family members, dying children, dying friends. Clearly Julian had known the rare gift of standing with those who are in pain and the spiritual communion of shared suffering.

These revelations were shown to a simple, uneducated creature[5] in the year of our Lord 1373, on the eighth day of May[6]; she had already asked God for three gifts: the first was vivid perception of his Passion, the second was bodily sickness in youth at thirty years of age, the third was for God to give her three wounds.[7]

LT 2, P. 42

I thought how I wished I had been there at the crucifixion with Mary Magdalene and with others who were Christ's dear friends,[8] and therefore I longed to be shown him in the flesh so that I might have more knowledge of our Savior's bodily suffering and of our Lady's fellow-suffering and that of all his true friends who then saw his pain; I wanted to be one of them and suffer with him.[9]

LT 2, P. 42

10 From the early days of the church, the faithful had been taught to pray for a holy death and always to be mindful of their mortality. Death and dying were a constant presence in the Middle Ages; even young children were likely to have seen a dead body. So the practices of imagining one's death and preparing for it were important ways of remembering the transitory nature of earthly life.

11 These rites included a final confession of sin, absolution, anointing with oil that had been blessed for that use, and a final communion with consecrated bread. All these rites of the church's normative sacramental life extended to the dying person a sign of Christ's love, forgiveness, and welcome at the time of death.

12 Julian requested that she be brought to the point of death. She desired to know as fully as possible the moment of complete dependency upon God's grace and mercy and the truth of letting go of all that is earthly life.

13 Here Julian qualifies her request, recognizing her human limitations and asking that her prayer not be contrary to God's will for her. Her insights into this dynamic of creature and creator come into play again and again as she is mindful of her own small, finite life. While never servile, Julian is humble in the best sense. She knows that her mind, heart, and body dwell within time and space, and that her human understanding is not equal to God's.

14 These three wounds—contrition, compassion, and earnest longing—speak of Julian's own hunger for God's presence and self-disclosure. Her longing is a gift, a homing instinct, a yearning for the One in whom she lives and moves and has her being.

The second gift came to me with contrition: I longed eagerly to be on my death-bed,[10] so that I might in that sickness receive all the rites of Holy Church,[11] that I might myself believe I was dying and that everyone who saw me might believe the same, for I wanted no hopes of earthly life.[12]

LT 2, P. 43

I longed for these two things—the Passion and the sickness—with one reservation, saying, "Lord, you know what I would have if it is your will that I should have it; and if it is not your will, good Lord, do not be displeased, for I only want what you want."[13]

LT 2, P. 43

As for the third gift, by the grace of God and the teaching of Holy Church, I conceived a great longing to receive three wounds in my life: that is to say, the wound of true contrition, the wound of kind compassion, and the wound of an earnest longing for God. And this last petition was with no reservation.[14]

LT 2, P. 43

15 Julian's prayer was answered; she contracted an illness that seemed to be fatal. She and her mother thought her last moments had come and the final good-byes were said.

16 In some ways, Julian's account sounds like a near-death experience. Her desire to be with God grew stronger, and she consented to her own dying.

17 Julian accepts what appear to be her final moments, in essence saying "yes" to the movement toward death. While it may appear at this point in the text that she is saying that God sent the illness, her subsequent reflections make it clear that God's mercy and goodness would make that impossible. God is with her, but God does not will her suffering.

18 Looking upon the cross brings consolation, for in beholding the suffering of Jesus, Julian knows that Jesus is with her in suffering. Intimately and tenderly, he reveals God's immeasurable love.

And when I was thirty and a half years old, God sent me a bodily sickness in which I lay for three days and three nights; and on the fourth night I received all the rites of Holy Church and did not believe that I would live until morning. And after this I lingered on for two days and two nights. And on the third night I often thought that I was dying and so did those who were with me.[15]

LT 3, P. 44

I wanted to live so as to love God better and for longer, and therefore know and love him better in the bliss of heaven. For it seemed to me that all the short time I had lived here was as nothing compared with that heavenly bliss.[16] So I thought, "Good Lord, may my ceasing to live be by your glory!" And I understood, both with my reason and by the bodily pains I felt, that I was dying. And I fully accepted the will of God with all the will of my heart.[17]

LT 3, P. 44

My parish priest was sent for to be present at my death, and by the time he came my eyes were fixed and I could not speak. He set the cross before my face and said, "I have brought you the image of your Maker and Savior. Look upon it and be comforted."[18]

LT 3, P. 44

19 Julian's book is full of references to sight—looking, beholding, seeing, and gazing. The sacred encounter with Jesus occurs in and through this beholding of the crucifix. Julian looked straight at the crucifix, in part out of physical weakness; she does not look heavenward, but directly in front of her. This suggestion of complete focus continues in the text, as she reminds the reader that the living God is right in front of us, dwelling within all that is confusing, disorienting, frightening, and painful.

20 To Julian, the crucifix is not ugly. It bears the image of a man dying, with nails in his hands and feet, yet it has its own beauty and integrity despite the fiends who surround it.

21 As Julian's condition becomes more serious and her breathing labored, she begins to anticipate her own end.

22 As suddenly as the sickness has come, the process of dying is mysteriously reversed. No medicine or treatment has brought about this marvelous alteration. Wellness comes to her with breath, with the easing of pain, with her own marveling.

23 Julian desires to remember the Passion of Jesus. The practice of *anamnesis* (literally, "against forgetting"), so central to Christian sacramental life, leads the faithful to call to mind all of God's works of mercy and love, especially as revealed in the life and ministry of Jesus. In the early church, forgetting was a primordial sin, a way of failing to be fully human. When we forget our true nature, and fail to be grateful for all we have received, our perceptions are distorted and our actions self-centered.

24 Julian desired to be with Jesus in his suffering, to accompany him out of love and gratefulness. Her desire springs from her nature as one made in the image and likeness of God, the fruit of a "naturally kind soul." This desire is known in compassionate human interaction, when we are present to one another in pain and sorrow.

I consented to fix my eyes on the face of the crucifix if I could, and so I did, because I thought that I might be able to bear looking straight ahead for longer than I could manage to look upwards.[19]

LT 3, P. 44

Everything except the cross was ugly to me, as if crowded with fiends.[20] After this the upper part of my body began to die to such an extent that I had almost no feeling and was short of breath. And then I truly believed that I had died.[21] And at this moment, all my suffering was suddenly taken from me, and I seemed to be as well, especially in the upper part of my body, as ever I was before. I marveled at this sudden change, for it seemed to me a mysterious work of God, not a natural one.[22]

LT 3, P. 45

Then it suddenly occurred to me that I should entreat our Lord graciously to give me the second wound, so that my whole body should be filled with remembrance and feeling of his blessed Passion;[23] for I wanted his pains to be my pains, with compassion, and then longing for God. Yet in this I never asked for a bodily sight or showing of God, but for fellow-suffering, such as a naturally kind soul might feel for our Lord Jesus; he was willing to become a mortal man for love, so I wanted to suffer with him.[24]

LT 3, P. 45

25 While she is still severely weakened, Julian is granted a graphic vision of Jesus's blood—"hot and fresh and plentiful." She witnesses a horrific dying, fully represented in the bleeding and the pain. How can it be that the man Jesus is also fully divine, so that God is present in this bleeding and suffering? This is the moment that leads her to see that Jesus embraces her suffering, and the suffering of all humanity.

26 In this "showing" of Jesus on the cross, Julian also sees the fullness of the Trinity: Father, Son, and Holy Spirit. All in a moment, God's self-disclosure is known to her. She sees and knows that this is the life of the Trinity, and that leads her to rejoice. God's everlasting desire for friendship and communion is revealed in and through the sight of Jesus on the cross. Julian is led to perceive the divine mercy and kindness that infuse every aspect of human life. "Jesus" becomes code for "Holy Trinity" because Jesus reveals the Three in One, and One in Three.

Then I suddenly saw the red blood trickling down from under the crown of thorns, hot and fresh and very plentiful, as though it were the moment of his Passion when the crown of thorns was thrust onto his blessed head, he who was both God and man, the same who suffered for me like that. I believe truly and strongly that it was he himself who showed me this, without any intermediary.[25]

LT 4, P. 45

And as part of the same showing the Trinity suddenly filled my heart with the greatest joy. And I understood that in heaven it will be like that for ever for those who come there. For the Trinity is God, God is the Trinity; the Trinity is our maker and protector, the Trinity is our dear friend for ever, our everlasting joy and bliss, through our Lord Jesus Christ. And this was shown in the first revelation and in all of them; for it seems to me that where Jesus is spoken of, the Holy Trinity is to be understood.[26]

LT 4, P. 46

27 "Our blessed Lady," Mary, the mother of Jesus, stayed with her son as he died, and the religious art of this time often depicted Mary kneeling at the foot of the cross, beholding her son. This image is of great comfort to those mothers whose children have died.

28 Medieval devotional practice led the faithful to imagine viewing Jesus's death both as human and as fully divine. The Virgin Mary, as an archetype of contemplative awareness and practice, was understood to discern the fullness of God's revelation in her son on the cross.

29 Julian makes it clear that her intent in writing down her revelations is to direct the reader's attention to God. She is an instrument of God's will, always pointing beyond herself to the God she serves.

30 She is convinced that her visions came because God trusted her to hand on her insights to others. The visions and her subsequent twenty years of reflection and prayer are not a private exchange. While deeply personal, they are intended to feed the community of the faithful, as they have for many centuries. Throughout the text Julian emphasizes God's infinite goodness and generosity, which is why her showings are intended for all, as a way of knowing the divine mercy, kindness, and love in the midst of turmoil and devastation.

31 This work, while theologically sophisticated, is intended for anyone who needs reassurance, succor, and encouragement.

Then he brought our blessed Lady into my mind. I saw
her spiritually in bodily likeness, a meek and simple maid,
young—little more than a child, of the same bodily form as
when she conceived.[27] God also showed me part of the wisdom and truth of her soul, so that I understood with what
reverence she beheld her God and Maker, and how reverently she marveled that he chose to be born of her, a simple
creature of his own making.[28]

LT 4, P. 46

I beg you all for God's sake and advise you for your own
advantage that you stop paying attention to the poor being
to whom this vision was shown, and eagerly, attentively
and humbly contemplate God,[29] who in his gracious love
and eternal goodness wanted the vision to be generally
known to comfort us all; for it is God's will that you should
receive it with joy and pleasure as great as if Jesus had
shown it to you all.[30]

LT 8, P. 53

I am not saying this to the wise, for they know it well; but
I am saying it to those of you who are ignorant, to support
and comfort you: we all need support.[31]

LT 9, PP. 53–54

32   "Knowledge" here means not only information, but knowing in the sense of acquaintance, befriending, and shared experience. Over time, as we come to know God and ourselves, we know ourselves to be loved by the One who makes, loves, and cares for us.

33   When sloth, one of the seven deadly sins, takes hold of the soul, a kind of spiritual inertia ensues. Sloth can be brought about by spiritual and physical fatigue, a sense of hopelessness that is made worse by isolation and loneliness. Sloth leads away from a dedicated, creative life as we bog down yet fail to ask for help.

34   The second kind of sickness, despair, is more enervating than sloth, and it often visits the soul when immediate circumstances have delivered a terrible shock. All seems dark and hopeless; any awareness of love and mercy recedes and disappears.

We need to have three kinds of knowledge: the first is
to know our Lord God; the second is to know ourselves,
what we are through him in nature and grace; the third is
to know humbly what we ourselves are where our sin and
weakness are concerned. And, as I understand it, the entire
showing was made for these three.[32]

LT 72, pp. 160–161

God showed that we suffer from two kinds of sickness: one
of them is impatience or sloth, because we find our trouble
and suffering a heavy burden to bear,[33] and the other is
despair, or doubtful fear, as I shall explain later.[34]

LT 73, p. 161

35 Throughout the showings, Julian hears the divine voice say, "It is I." This echoes the voice from the burning bush that tells Moses, when he asks for the divine name, "I am who I am" (Exodus 3:13–15), and the "I am" sayings of Jesus in the Gospel of John ("I am the light of the world." "I am the good shepherd."). Julian comes to know only life, love, and light through the visions of the bleeding Christ. The cheerful and gracious self-offering of divine life for the whole universe ran contrary to the medieval theology of atonement, in which Jesus, God's Son, is offered up on the cross to appease divine wrath for sin. In Julian's world this particular atonement theology was widely held. Her strong and sturdy affirmation is that the Trinity is a unity of persons, in which Father, Son, and Holy Spirit indwell one another fully and lovingly. As we shall see, she discerns that contrary to the widely held view of substitutionary atonement, there can "be no anger in God" (LT 13, p. 61).

36 In Jesus, God becomes "familiar," our kin. Julian next speaks of God's "courtesy," evoking the ritualized behaviors of respect and mutual honoring of feudal society. Just as paintings of the Annunciation from this period often showed Gabriel bowing in courtesy to Mary, Julian senses that God is ever bowing before us, courteously offering friendship and aid. As we are enlightened by these showings, we are formed by divine courtesy and kindness without end. Our human life becomes infused by the life, love, and light of the divine love shown forth on the cross.

37 Julian refers repeatedly to God's goodness. According to scholastic theology, there can be no evil in God; rather, goodness and God are synonymous. Thus God brings forth all goodness, and eventually all goodness that has gone forth from God returns to God, sustained by divine life, love, and light. Julian's view of human nature endows us with an inherent capacity to see and know God's presence. While we cannot know God fully, we have been given the power to reason and thus to recognize and receive God's teaching and guiding. We can certainly misunderstand or refuse God's will, but Julian believes we have been created in such a way that we may understand and experience this "sweet harmony" between God and our reason.

I was able to touch, see and feel some of the three properties of God on which the strength and meaning of the whole revelation is based, and they were seen in every showing and most characteristically in the twelfth, where it often says, "It is I." The properties are these: life, love and light.[35] There is marvelous familiarity in life, gracious courtesy in love, and in light there is endless kindness. These properties belonged to a single goodness; and my reason desired to unite and cling to this goodness with all its might.[36] I watched with reverent fear, marveling greatly as I saw and felt the sweet harmony between our reason and God, understanding that it is the highest gift we have received and that it is grounded in nature.[37]

LT 83, P. 176

1 God's "familiar" love, the love of father, mother, sibling, and spouse, permeates Julian's reflections. The word "homely" in Middle English suggests something known in a domestic, familial context. Julian's experience of the showings, and her subsequent reflections, lead her to assure her readers that God is close to us and our daily domestic routines.

2 Because Norwich was a textile center, it was natural for Julian to speak of clothing when evoking our bodily life and the life of commerce in Norwich. To imagine God as our clothing is to convey closeness, as skin next to cloth. It also conveys interconnection and relationship. Our clothing embraces all of our bodies, both what we wear for daily public display and what is hidden from view. Julian suggests that we are clothed with God's own self, wrapped and enfolded in love.

3 The hazelnut was a common food at this time, so the image would convey something homely and ordinary to the reader.

4 In this vision of the hazelnut lying in the palm of one hand, Julian is given an inspired sense of God's infinity that frames much of her reflections. God is to the created universe as Julian's hand is to the hazelnut. In other words, the whole of the created order—galaxies, suns, planets—is held within God's hand. This image also echoes a scriptural motif found in Isaiah 40:12: "Who has measured the waters in the hollow of his hand and marked off the heavens with a span, enclosed the dust of the earth in a measure, and weighed the mountains in scales and the hills in a balance?"

5 While beholding the littleness of all that is created, Julian cannot help but wonder how it continues to exist. How could it be that something so small is not obliterated? The answer she is given, while simple at first glance, is foundational to her theological reflections. This created universe lasts because God loves it into being and sustains it with love.

2 □ Images for God

At the same time, our Lord showed me a spiritual vision of
his familiar love.[1] I saw that for us he is everything that we
find good and comforting. He is our clothing, wrapping
us for love, embracing and enclosing us for tender love, so
that he can never leave us, being himself everything that is
good for us, as I understand it.[2]

LT 5, P. 47

In this vision he also showed a little thing, the size of a
hazelnut in the palm of my hand, and it was as round as a
ball.[3] I looked at it with my mind's eye and thought, "What
can this be?" And the answer came to me, "It is all that is
made."[4]

LT 5, P. 47

I wondered how it could last, for it was so small I thought
it might suddenly have disappeared. And the answer in my
mind was, "It lasts and will last for ever because God loves
it; and everything exists in the same way by the love of
God."[5]

LT 5, P. 47

21

6 As Julian beholds this little thing, she sees divine love: God makes, loves, and cares. All that is created has been brought forth in divine love, is sustained by that love, and will finally return to it. Thus all that is created is inherently good. God's own beauty and life infuse every aspect of the created order, which is cause for wonder and delight even though that creation is so very little compared to the immensity of God.

7 Julian's God-given yearning leads her to desire to fully know the One who has created her, loved her, cared for her. That desire, mirroring God's own longing for us, can only be satisfied by deeper love and unity with God. Note that her longing, while active and strong, has been examined. Knowing the strength of this desire, Julian discerns that trying to slake that thirst for God with anything that is less than God will always result in frustration. True happiness comes in knowing this holy desire for what it is, and seeking the giver.

8 Julian's theology is built around her awareness that we humans did not bring the creation into being. Her sense of God's presence and activity leads her toward a deepening perception of God's infinite and mysterious nature. She also affirms, again and again, that God has revealed God's own essence, which is love.

In this little thing I saw three properties: the first is that
God made it, the second is that God loves it, the third is
that God cares for it.[6] But what the maker, the carer and
the lover really is to me, I cannot tell; for until I become
one substance with him, I can never have complete rest or
true happiness; that is to say, until I am so bound to him
that there is no created thing between my God and me.[7]

LT 5, P. 47

We need to know the littleness of all created beings and to
set at nothing everything that is made in order to love and
possess God who is unmade.[8]

LT 5, P. 47

9 | As Julian describes her visions, in general, they fall into three catego-
ries. First, she lists "bodily sight," meaning those things that she saw
with her own eyes. Next, she indicates that she heard something
"inwardly"—words offered by the guidance of the Holy Spirit. Lastly,
she speaks of "spiritual sight," which is less easily explained than
bodily sight.

10 | This spiritual sight is hard for her to define, and doing so is both her
gift and her task. She spent twenty years reflecting on these visions,
allowing them to take part in a kind of inner conversation with each
other, and with God in prayer.

11 | Julian's long experience of taking care to receive the rich fullness of
the visions has led her to trust in the divine desire to teach, guide, and
lead us into the truth in love. She knows this takes time. She declares
her own shortcomings in communicating what she has learned, trusting in God's guidance both for her and for her readers.

12 | Notice that Julian desires clarity of vision. Here she echoes a theme
we find in Scripture: human beings suffer from spiritual "blindness,"
which today we would call ignorance, egotism, or self-centeredness.
Thus we cannot perceive things accurately until we turn toward God.
In turning toward our true destination and allowing it to draw us forward, we learn to let go of illusory goals and desires.

13 | The mutual longing of love that is the deepest truth of the divine-
human relationship leads us to behold God's light, life, and love. This
awakens our desire to seek God in all things, in all ways.

All this was shown in three ways: that is to say, by bodily sight, and by words formed in my understanding, and by spiritual sight.[9] But I neither can nor may show the spiritual vision as openly or as fully as I would like to.[10] But I trust that our Lord God almighty will out of his own goodness and love for you make you receive it more spiritually and more sweetly than I can or may tell it.[11]

LT 9, P. 54

I wished for better bodily sight to see it more clearly.[12] And I was answered in my reason, "If God wants to show you more, he will be your light. You need no light but him." For I saw him and sought him; for we are now so blind and so unwise that we never seek God until out of his goodness he shows himself to us, and if he graciously lets us see something of himself, then we are moved by the same grace to seek with a great longing to see him more fully; and thus I saw him and I sought him, I had him and I wanted him. And it seems to me that this is, or should be, our usual way of proceeding.[13]

LT 10, P. 55

1 Julian's counsel follows the traditional wisdom from Augustine of Hippo many centuries earlier: "Our hearts are restless until they rest in Thee."[1] The underlying theological anthropology holds that humanity is created *capax dei*, inherently "capable" of receiving and relating to the God who is our source and our end. We humans know who we are truly meant to be only when our primary frame of reference is this relationship to God. When other things—money, success, even human love—take the place of God, our lives are distorted and go awry.

2 The Genesis account of creation tells us that after God brought forth the creation, on the seventh day God rested. This motif of divine rest informs Hebraic and early Christian teaching about the Sabbath. We rest because God rested, and so that we may be restored and replenished, gently made new from the inside out. Julian knows this renewal to be the heart of contemplative practice and attention—the prayer that allows us to rest in God.

3 Julian affirms that God's self-disclosure takes place in time and space, so that we might know something of God, and might love more deeply and truly.

4 This kind of knowing comes through deep prayer, a prayer of quiet trust and gentle silence.

5 Our souls are made for the divine presence, and nothing can satisfy our deepest inner longings except God. When we settle for less, we become exhausted by our repeated attempts to quell the longing with inadequate substitutes.

6 Remember that Julian is not saying that we can rest only in God because God's creation is in some way inadequate, but is clarifying our high calling to be in loving relationship with God. Resting in God makes us truly human.

3 □ Our Relationship to God

This is the reason why we do not feel complete ease in our hearts and souls: we look here for satisfaction in things which are so trivial, where there is no rest to be found,[1] and do not know our God who is almighty, all wise, all good; he is rest itself.[2]

LT 5, P. 47

God wishes to be known,[3] and is pleased that we should rest in him;[4] for all that is below him does nothing to satisfy us; and this is why, until all that is made seems as nothing no soul can be at rest.[5] When a soul sets all at nothing for love, to have him who is everything, then he is able to receive spiritual rest.[6]

LT 5, P. 47

7 God, being infinitely kind and good, has made sure that we have what we need for our journey—most importantly, the truth of Jesus's Incarnation through which he embraced human life from the inside out. The church teaches that Jesus's humanity comes from his mother, Mary. As he was knit together in his mother's womb, so our humanity was revealed as good, beautiful, and destined for an intimate and tender relationship with God.

8 Julian is telling us that the divine goodness is a kind of medicine, which heals, restores, and makes the soul new. This goodness is constantly available to us through prayer.

9 Here she develops the imagery of God not only as close to us as our clothing, but also as like our very skin, our muscles, our ligaments, enclosing the inner organs. Her unapologetic use of bodily images confronts us with her radical sense of the truth of the Incarnation. In Jesus, God is telling us that every aspect of our physicality is hallowed by divine presence, created by divine will and joy, embraced by divine love. And she insists on this at a time when the people of Norwich would have seen bodies wracked by plague, dismembered by war, and starved by famine.

10 Divine love is a mystery, always beyond our full understanding. We may receive it, be healed by it, made new by it, and draw courage from it, yet never fully plumb the heights nor the depths of God's love.

11 Remember that Julian is writing this after her vision of Jesus bleeding and dying on the cross. She comes to this profound sense of comfort while embracing God's teaching: the Passion of Jesus points to the fullness of God's love for us. Enclosed in that love, we are "spiritually safe" even though our daily lives may be battered by circumstances beyond our control. Yet this vision of Jesus on the cross leads Julian to say that God is with us in the worst of times as well as the best, and knows our suffering intimately.

For in his goodness, God has ordained a great many excellent means to help us, of which the chief and principal one is the blessed Humanity which he took from the Virgin, with all the means which went before and come afterwards which belong to our redemption and our eternal salvation.[7]

LT 6, P. 49

The goodness of God is the highest object of prayers and it reaches down to our lowest need. It quickens our soul and gives it life, and makes it grow in grace and virtue.[8]

LT 6, P. 49

For as the body is clad in the cloth, and the flesh in the skin, and the bones in the flesh, and the heart in the chest, so are we, soul and body, clad in the goodness of God and enclosed in it.[9]

LT 6, P. 49

There is no being made that can know how much and how sweetly and how tenderly our Maker loves us.[10]

LT 6, P. 49

And what comforted me most in the vision was that our God and Lord, who is so holy and awe-inspiring, is also so familiar and courteous. And this was what gave me most happiness and the strongest sense of spiritual safety.[11]

LT 7, P. 51

12 Truly seeing our God and Lord entails seeing Jesus's suffering and death as a mysterious disclosure of divine kindness, mercy, and compassion. Julian perceives that Jesus's suffering on the cross is in some sense joyous—it witnesses to the love God bears us and God's desire to be intimately known to us.

13 Pay attention to Julian's verbs: God desires us to *long,* to *believe*, to *rejoice* and *take pleasure*, to *receive* comfort and support from God. Her initial visions and the fruit of her years of reflection have led her to a distinctive confidence and trust in God. We are made for this intimacy, which is an essential aspect of what she has been shown by the crucified Lord.

14 Julian echoes the words of Psalm 139: "If I take the wings of the morning and settle at the farthest limits of the sea, even there your hand shall lead me, and your right hand shall hold me fast." Even when we feel as though circumstances are drowning us God still keeps us safe, enclosed in love.

15 In the words of the Eastern Orthodox Church, "There is no place where God is not."

And truly and certainly this marvelous joy will be made known to all of us when we see him.[12] And this is what our Lord wants us to long for and believe, to rejoice and take pleasure in, to receive comfort and support from, as much as we can, until the time when we can see it for ourselves; for it seems to me that the greatest fullness of joy that we shall have is the marvelous courtesy and intimacy of the Father who made us, through our Lord Jesus Christ who is our brother and savior.[13]

LT 7, P. 51

At one moment my consciousness was taken down on to the sea bed, and there I saw green hills and valleys, looking as though they were covered in moss, with seaweed and sand. Then I understood this: that if a man or a woman were under the wide waters, if he could see God (and God is constantly with us) he would be safe, body and soul, and be unharmed, and furthermore, he would have more joy and comfort than words can say.[14]

LT 10, P. 55

And after this I saw God in an instant, that is to say, in my understanding, and in seeing this I saw that he is in everything.[15]

LT 11, P. 58

16 Throughout this passage God commands Julian *to see*. As a result of her visions, her insight is both cleansed and honed. She hears the invitation to see, to let go of willful ignorance and concepts too narrow for God's mercy and kindness. For if all has been ordered by God, "How can anything be amiss?" She reports this encounter with God as a test of her own soul, that she can come to trust that all God has made is providentially working for good.

17 This God and Lord, who is both familiar and courteous, thanks Julian for her own suffering. We don't know in detail what her suffering was, but this one sentence does tell us something beautiful and tender. God not only recognizes our own suffering and endures it with us, but also thanks us for our willingness.

18 Julian is not suggesting that God, like a magician, will remove all pain from our lives, but that God, who is in everything, protects us in the sense of keeping our souls safe. When we practice focusing both on the present moment and on what is timeless, it reminds us that no one escapes suffering in the long run. The spiritual task is finding a way to walk through and with suffering, entrusting all to God.

19 Like any wise parent, God gives us the freedom to make errors in judgment, to grow from experience, to try again.

20 When we fall, God is with us. Through falling we are led to increasing wisdom and insight, to honesty about what has happened, and to ask for guidance from God and our spiritual companions. And when we call upon the divine mercy, wisdom, and tenderness, it gives God the opportunity to be more fully known and loved. In a similar way, when we call upon a friend for help, that friend is known in a new way and the friendship is strengthened.

21 Here Julian muses on her own visions. What God has shown her draws her more deeply into love for both God and neighbor. In writing her manuscript, she hands on what she has received.

And God showed all this most gloriously, with this meaning, "See that I am God. See that I am in everything. See that I do everything. See that I have never stopped ordering my works, nor ever shall, eternally. See that I lead everything on to the conclusion I ordained for it before time began, by the same power of wisdom and love with which I made it. How can anything be amiss?" Thus powerfully, wisely and lovingly was the soul tested in this vision. Then I saw truly that I must comply with great reverence, rejoicing in God.[16]

LT 11, P. 59

After this our good Lord said, "I thank you for your suffering, especially in your youth."[17]

LT 14, P. 62

God wishes us to know that he safely protects us in both sorrow and joy equally.[18]

LT 15, P. 64

And he allows us to fall;[19] and in his blessed love we are preserved by his strength and wisdom; and through mercy and grace we are raised to a greater abundance of joys.[20] And thus God wants to be known and loved now and forever in his righteousness and in his mercy. And the soul that truly sees this through grace takes pleasure in both and rejoices without end.[21]

LT 35, P. 90

22 God intends that we have the wisdom, understanding, and insight needed for our short time span on the earth.

23 There is also much that is beyond our comprehension. Julian ruminates on the essence of any revelation, which is to show forth and hide at the same time. Her years of considering the gift of the showings have led her to know this well. She has the insight and understanding to know how much is beyond her grasp.

24 Although the ways of God are often hidden from us, because of God's kindness we are never to believe that evil, pain, and sorrow are the last word.

25 Julian invites us to the practice of trust. When life's storms bring us low, she reminds us that God is ever with us. Not only that, she points us toward hope in the midst of chaos.

26 Over time, Julian sees that sin is rooted in our failure to love as God loves, which is known to her through her visions of Jesus on the cross.

27 At a time when much devotional art depicted the final judgment as a horrific event, with many souls consigned to hell-fire and eternal torture, Julian stands firm. Her faith assures her readers that God's judgment does not look like that. The righteousness of God goes hand in hand with divine mercy and kindness.

And in this I saw that God does not want us to be afraid
of knowing the things that he shows us; he shows them
because he wants us to know them, and through this knowledge he wants us to love him and be happy and rejoice
in him for ever.[22] And because of his great love for us he
shows us everything which it is valuable and useful for us
to know in this world;[23] and the things which he wants
to remain a mystery for the time being, he nevertheless
because of his great kindness, shows us in a veiled way, and
from this showing he wants us to believe and understand
that we shall really see them in his everlasting bliss.[24]

LT 36, P. 91

This then is what he intends: he does not want us to be
brought too low by the storms and sorrows that befall us,
for it has always been so before the coming of a miracle.[25]

LT 36, P. 93

Failure of love on our part is the only cause of all our
suffering.[26]

LT 37, P. 94

God judges us in terms of our natural essence, which is
always preserved unchanged in him, whole and safe for
ever; and this judgment comes from his righteousness.[27]

LT 45, P. 106

28 This is an astounding statement, given the medieval view of judgment. After years of reviewing the showings, and carefully testing her own perceptions, Julian concludes that God does not blame us. As we will see, this idea brings tension, for what does that say about sin and evil?

29 On the one hand, Julian has been shown that there is no anger or blame in God. On the other, she lives with the church's teaching that our sins and misdoings are all known to God, and that we deserve just punishment. She struggles to hold to both truths, seeing that there are different "levels" of judgment.

The first judgment, from God's righteousness, comes from his exalted, everlasting love, and this is the kind and lovely judgment which was shown throughout the precious revelation in which I saw him assign us no kind of blame.[28] And though this was sweet and delectable, yet I could not be quite freed from anxiety just by contemplating this, because of the judgment of Holy Church, which I had understood before and of which I was always aware. And according to this judgment it seemed to me that I had to acknowledge myself a sinner, and by the same judgment I understood that sinners deserve blame and anger one day; and I could see no blame and anger in God, and then I felt a longing greater than I can or may tell; for God himself revealed the higher judgment at the same time, and therefore I was bound to accept it; and the lower judgment had been taught me before by Holy Church and therefore I could in no way abandon the lower judgment.[29]

LT 45, P. 106

30   We have the capacity to know ourselves, but if we honestly reflect on our behavior we know that sometimes we baffle ourselves. This passage sounds a lot like Paul's letter to the Romans: "I do not understand my own actions. For I do not do what I want, but I do the very thing I hate" (Romans 7:15).

31   Julian senses that over time, as we become more open to divine love and mercy, our way of knowing and seeing is made new by God.

32   In seeking to know ourselves in this way, we may discover the eternal assurance of our being of God's making, sustaining, caring. Julian wants her evenchristen to recover the identity first bestowed on us in our creation and fully restored to us in the Incarnation. Thus she encourages anyone reading the text to embrace an identity gifted by God.

33   Our task is to seek to know ourselves as God does, being completely honest about our sins and short-comings, while being mindful of the "everlasting joy" that is always awaiting us.

34   How can there be anger in God, who is known through mercy and whose infinite goodness is the well from which all creation springs? And how can there be forgiveness, which is not necessary if there is no anger in God? Julian's theology is utterly distinctive for her time. Because of her unshakable sense of God's love and goodness, she has been led to the awareness that there is no anger in God. It follows that, without anger, forgiveness becomes superfluous.

We may have knowledge of ourselves in this life through the continuing help and strength of our higher nature, a knowledge which we may develop and increase with the help and encouragement of mercy and grace,[30] but we can never know ourselves completely until the last moment, the moment in which this transitory life and customary grief and pain will come to an end.[31] And therefore it is right and proper for us both by nature and by grace to long and to pray with all our might to know ourselves in the fullness of everlasting joy.[32]

LT 46, P. 107

And from all that I saw it seemed to me that it was necessary for us to see and to acknowledge that we are sinners; we do many evil things which we ought not to do and leave undone many good deeds which we ought to do, and for this we deserve punishment and anger.[33] And in spite of all this I saw truly that our Lord was never angry and never will be angry, for he is God: goodness, life, truth, love, peace; and his loving-kindness does not allow him to be angry, nor does his unity; for I saw truly that it is against the nature of strength to be angry, and against the nature of his wisdom and against the nature of his goodness. God is the goodness that cannot be angry, for he is nothing but goodness, and in God's eyes there can be neither anger nor forgiveness between him and our soul; for through his own goodness our soul is completely united with God, so that nothing can come between God and the soul.[34]

LT 46, P. 108

35 Coming to know ourselves as well as possible, we begin to notice when we despair and when we lean toward careless behaviors. Julian, enclosed in her anchorage for years, had spent much time in study, prayer, and silence. Her own contemplative practice has brought her to trust in this God who is only goodness.

36 Here Julian's bifocal way of seeing again comes into play. We cannot see as God does. Her words remind us of Isaiah's text: "For my thoughts are not your thoughts, nor are your ways my ways, says the Lord" (Isaiah 55:8).

37 Julian makes a case for honest, self-effacing appraisal of our own lives and behaviors. This is made possible as we grow in the confidence of God's great kindness. We may be vulnerable, frank with ourselves and with God about our misdeeds. Thus we may examine our behavior without fear in the light of God's love.

We should not on the one hand fall too low, inclining to despair, nor on the other hand be too reckless as if we did not care, but should recognize our own weakness without concealment, knowing that we cannot stand even for the twinkling of an eye unless we are protected by grace.[35] We should cling reverently to God, trusting in him alone; for man and God regard things in two quite different ways; it is proper for man humbly to accuse himself, and it is proper for God in his natural goodness kindly to excuse him.[36]

LT 52, PP. 126–127

And the way our Lord wants us to accuse ourselves is this: earnestly and truly seeing and recognizing our fall and all the troubles that come from it, seeing and knowing that we can never make it good, but at the same time we should earnestly and truly see and know the everlasting love which he has for us, and his abundant mercy. And seeing and knowing both together in this way is the humble self-accusation which our Lord asks of us, and where it exists, he himself has brought it about.[37]

LT 52, P. 127

38 Julian understands that in Adam's fall and exile from paradise, our true state is revealed. And because in Jesus we participate in divinity, Adam's fall is known and experienced by Jesus. This teaching from the first centuries of church doctrine offers a stunning insight: through Jesus's Incarnation, God embraces every aspect of human existence, including the fall of Adam. There is nothing that is outside the realm of this divine embrace. In taking on Adam's fall, moreover, God also takes on the burden of our own confusion, sadness, despair, and sin.

39 Julian's own process of understanding involves reason and prayer, using her inherent gifts of memory, reason, skill, and intelligence to interpret her showings. She also listens deeply to the Bible and to church teaching. Some scholars have commented that her process is informed by the Benedictine practice of *lectio divina,* the slow, meditative reading of Scripture.

40 Julian affirms the essential goodness of humanity, made in the image and likeness of God. Divine mercy and grace, the most important nutrients for human goodness, create renewed joy. In other words, God is on our side in every way.

And I saw that God wants us to recognize that he does not take the fall of any human being that shall be saved more harshly than he took the fall of Adam, who we know was eternally loved and securely protected in the time of his need, and is now blissfully compensated with great surpassing joys; for our Lord God is so good, so noble, so generous that he can never blame anyone who will be blessed and praised in the end.[38]

LT 53, P. 128

I had some degree of insight into this, and it is a process grounded in nature, that is to say, our reason is grounded in God, who is the summit of essential being.[39] From this essential nature, mercy and grace spring and spread into us, influencing all things in fulfillment of our joy. These are the grounds in which we grow and reach our fulfillment, for in nature we have our life and our being, and in mercy and grace we have our growth and our fulfillment; nature, mercy and grace are three aspects of a single goodness, and where one works they all work in the things which concern us in this life.[40]

LT 56, P. 134

41　As we become more closely united to God, our desire to honor God's trust in us grows. Praise and thanksgiving become habitual.

42　God's work within the human soul heals us and restores our capacity for love.

43　God's relationship with us is one of parenthood. God is father to us because our nature is essentially of God, and mother because we are brought forth from God's own being. The love and goodness of the Holy Ghost nurture and form us.

44　Our relationship to God is also spousal, as bride is united to bridegroom. Julian may be thinking of New Testament texts in which the community of believers has become the bride of Jesus, an image of oneness that was also important to the teachings of the early church.

45　Medieval preachers often interpreted events like plague and famine as God's just punishment for sinful men and women. For Julian, the fear caused by this theology made truly knowing God's love impossible. Here she explores the difference between the kind of fear that causes us to turn to God for help and mercy, and the fear that sees God as harsh and full of wrath, the image of an angry taskmaster. Julian advises us to examine our own fears—do they arise out of a distorted point of view? If so, they are inhibiting a relationship of love and grace.

By the power of the same precious union we love our Maker and please him, praise him, thank him and endlessly rejoice in him.[41] And this work that goes on continually in every soul that shall be saved is the godly will mentioned previously.[42] And so in our making, God almighty is our father by nature; and God all wisdom is our mother by nature, along with the love and goodness of the Holy Ghost; and these are all one God, one Lord.[43] And in this binding and union he is a real and true bridegroom, and we his loved bride and his fair maiden, a bride with whom he is never displeased; for he says, "I love you and you love me, and our love shall never be divided."[44]

LT 58, p. 137

The fear which makes us quickly flee from all that is not good and fall upon our Lord's breast like a child upon its mother's bosom, which makes us do this with all our mind and with all our will-power, knowing our feebleness and our great need, knowing God's everlasting goodness and his blessed love, seeking salvation only in him and clinging to him with sure trust—the fear which makes us do this is natural, gracious, good and true. And everything contrary to this is either completely wrong or partly wrong.[45]

LT 74, pp. 163–164

46 Out of love and pity God continually yearns for us. Julian describes God's longing for humanity as an unquenchable thirst, the thirst she sees in Jesus as he bleeds on the cross.

47 God's love-longing is personal; God desires to teach and lead each person in a way that is "fitting and beneficial."

48 When we have reached the end of our lives, we are drawn into God's "bliss." Julian's vision of what awaits us after death differs strongly from the medieval depictions of the end of life, with many souls being thrown into everlasting pain and suffering.

49 At the end of time the bliss that God desires to give "all those who will be saved" will encounter our deepest yearnings, and in that meeting, all of our residual suffering and distress will be healed.

50 Julian senses that God's goodness, which is beyond our imagination, wells up within us *and* flows into us. She also alludes to a readiness to receive this goodness; in God's time, with our consent, we will be made able to receive.

I saw that God can do all that is necessary for us; and these three are necessary: love, longing and pity. Pity in love protects us in our time of need, and longing in the same love draws us up to heaven; for God's thirst is to draw mankind in general up into himself, and in this thirst he has drawn up the holy ones who are now in bliss; and to get the living, he is always drawing and drinking, yet he still thirsts and longs.[46]

LT 75, P. 164

I saw three kinds of longing in God, and all to one end; and we have the same longing in us, and of the same power, and to the same end. The first is that he longs to teach us to know him and love him for evermore, as is fitting and beneficial for us.[47] The second is that he longs to have us up in his bliss, as souls are when they are taken out of suffering into heaven.[48] The third is to fill us with bliss; and that longing shall be fulfilled on the final day, to last for ever; for I saw, as our faith assures us, that suffering and sorrow will end for all those who will be saved.[49] And not only shall we receive the same bliss which the souls before us have had in heaven, but we shall also receive new bliss which will flow into us abundantly out of God and fill us; and this is the good which he has ordained that we should be given since before time began. This good is treasured up and hidden in himself; for until that time, no being is able or deserves to receive it.[50]

LT 75, P. 165

51 The magnanimous love of God leaves us awestruck. Such fear is not suffering, but the awe that is at the heart of adoration, leading us to marvel and to wonder.

52 Continuing to walk in a way of faith, hope, and love, seeking to discover the depths of divine goodness and kindness, inevitably leads us to union with God—what Julian calls "the right way."

53 Here Julian makes characteristic use of the word "friend" for God. Her belief that God comes to us as a friend and desires this kind of bond with us is one of her most striking insights. Her insights echo the Wisdom of Solomon: "In every generation she [Wisdom] passes into holy souls and makes them friends of God, and prophets" (Wisdom 7:27b).

54 Because none of us lives without sinning, we need to grow in our capacity to recognize sin, to name it, and to amend our behavior. Otherwise we may become incapable of resisting sin and fall into "torment," which for Julian is feeling separated from God.

55 Julian continually offers hope to her readers. Whenever we despair over our own behavior, her "remedy" is to acknowledge it truthfully and turn toward God for help and instruction.

But this kind of trembling and fear will bring no suffering, for it befits the noble might of God thus to be seen by his creatures, as they tremble fearfully and quake with meekness of joy, marveling at the greatness of God the Maker and the littleness of all that is made; for seeing this will make all created beings marvelously meek and mild.[51] Therefore God wants us to know and recognize this, and it befits us to do so, both by nature and by grace, to long for his sight and for this to happen, because it leads us in the right way and keeps us in the true life and unites us to God.[52]

LT 75, P. 165

The wisdom is for people to behave according to the wishes and advice of their greatest and most supreme friend.[53]

LT 76, P. 166

And so it is God's will that we recognize sin, and pray earnestly and work hard and humbly seek for guidance so that we do not fall into it [sin] blindly; and if we fall, that we rise again quickly, for turning from God through sin even for a moment is the greatest torment a soul can ever suffer.[54]

LT 76, P. 166

This is the remedy, then: that we should acknowledge our sinfulness and flee to our Lord, for the readier we are to do this, the more it will profit us to approach him.[55]

LT 77, P. 168

56 We are reminded that the whole of the showings, and of Julian's reflections, takes place at the foot of the cross, in the company of the friends who do not leave Jesus in his last hours. This moment defines friendship as constant, even in the worst moments.

57 Jesus cautions us against judging ourselves "unreasonably," as if all our pain and suffering were our own fault. Instead, we should be realistic about our shortcomings and work on those—"a profitable penance"—instead of worrying about things we can't change.

58 The eternal friendship extended by God is spoken of by Jesus in the Gospel of John: "This is my commandment, that you love one another as I have loved you. No one has greater love than this, to lay down one's life for one's friends. You are my friends if you do what I command you" (John 15:12–14).

For when we remember his blessed Passion, with pity and love, then we suffer with him as his friends did who saw it, and this was shown in the thirteenth revelation, near the beginning, where it speaks of pity;[56] for he says, "Do not accuse yourself overmuch, claiming that your tribulation and woe is all your own fault. I do not want you to be unreasonably sad and sorrowful; for I tell you that you will suffer woe whatever you do. And therefore I want you to recognize clearly what your penance is, and then you will truly see that your whole life is a profitable penance."[57]

LT 77, P. 168

Let us fly to our Lord and we shall be comforted, touch him and we shall be made clean, cling to him and we shall be safe and secure from all manner of peril; for our courteous Lord wants us to be as friendly with him as the heart may conceive or the soul may desire.[58]

LT 77, PP. 168–169

59 Julian tells us we are grounded in God. All comes forth from God. Nothing exists that does not have its origin in God, for without God, nothing could have being.

60 Sin has a destructive force, from which we need divine protection. In our weakness, we need God's mercy and love to protect us from our self-destructive and even violent habits.

61 God is not hands-off. Julian speaks of "courtesy," evoking feudal patterns of honoring one's lord. In this case, the Lord is honoring us with kind courtesy, offering merciful protection by helping us to see the ways in which our actions hurt ourselves and one another.

62 Julian states repeatedly that God is united with us, and she is shown the truth of this as she beholds Jesus on the cross. Divine life and human life are one. As this awareness takes hold of us, we can sometimes see a pressing problem from a new perspective and sense God's desire to cleanse our sight. The steadfast love of God remains unchanging, no matter how long it takes us to recognize our dilemmas.

63 Julian's lighthearted humility lets her see that none of us is perfect and none of us escapes falling into sinful behavior. But as we learn to take ourselves less seriously, to confess readily and seek help, we discover God in the midst of our confusion and delusion.

64 Julian contends that the only true way to know ourselves is to see ourselves, like the hazelnut, held in God's hand, "tenderly protected." When we fall into the habit of seeing ourselves otherwise, we are already telling ourselves a deeply destructive lie. When we imagine ourselves to be alienated from God, or hidden from God, we delude ourselves. This "highest truth" comes from God.

It is his wish that we should have knowledge of four things: the first is that he is the ground from which we have all our life and our being;[59] the second, that he protects us mightily and mercifully in the time of our sin and among all the enemies that fall upon us so fiercely—and we are in the greater peril because we give them the opportunity and do not know our own need;[60] the third is that he protects us with kind courtesy and lets us know that we are going wrong;[61] the fourth is how steadfastly he waits for us with unchanging face, for he wants us to turn to him and unite with him in love, as he is united with us.[62]

LT 78, P. 169

If there be any lover of God on earth who is continuously kept from falling, I do not know of it, for it was not shown to me.[63] But this was shown: that in falling and in rising we are always tenderly protected in one love; for as God beholds us we do not fall, and as we behold ourselves we do not stand, and both these seem to me to be true, but our Lord God's view is the highest truth; so we are much indebted to God for showing us this great truth while we are still in this earthly life.[64]

LT 82, PP. 175–176

65   The showings that Julian received never gave her any sense of divine wrath or desire for retribution. Instead, she was given a full and rich sequence of images that spoke profoundly of immeasurable love. God does recognize evil and stands fully against it. At the same time, God being God, to act out of anger is impossible. Such an action would be inconsistent with God's own being, which is infinite love beyond our powers of imagination.

66   The prevailing theology of Julian's time instructed faithful Christians to confess their personal sins and undertake acts of penance as a way to allay God's anger over their shortcomings. While Julian had been formed by the medieval church's way of viewing sin, her visions run completely counter to what she has been taught. There is no anger in God, and what we might perceive as divine anger is our own emotional state that we have projected onto God.

67   Julian reminds us that failing to see God leads us to fail and to fall. When we cannot accurately see the truth about ourselves and one another, our perceptions become faulty and distorted. Then our subsequent patterns of behavior are inconsistent with God's hopes for us. We become especially aware of this drastic gap between God's desires for us and our own distorted views when we behave in ways that hurt ourselves and others.

But it seems to me that there can be no anger in God, for our good Lord is always thinking of his own glory and the good of all who shall be saved. With power and justice he stands up against the reprobates who out of wickedness and malignity work hard to plot and act against God's will.[65]

LT 13, P. 61

I understood that the mercy of God would be the remission of his anger after our time of sin; for I thought that to a soul whose whole intention and desire is to love, the anger of God would be harsher than any other punishment, and therefore I took it that the remission of his anger would be one of the principal points of his mercy. But however hard I looked and longed, I could not see this anywhere in the whole showing.[66]

LT 47, P. 109

Mercy works through tenderness and grace blended with abundant pity; for by the work of mercy we are held safe and by the work of mercy everything is turned to good for us. Through love mercy allows us to fail to some extent, and in so far as we fail, so far we fall, and in so far as we fall, so far we die; for we really must die in so far as we fail to see and feel God who is our life.[67]

LT 48, P. 111

68 Here Julian offers an astounding insight: if God cannot be angry, then logically God cannot forgive. Her long years of reflecting and pondering have led her to make a statement that continues to startle her readers. God's loving nature rules out both anger and forgiveness. Julian is not saying human beings don't need to forgive one another, but she does claim that God's nature is love beyond our comprehension or experience.

Now this was a great marvel to the soul, continually shown in everything and considered with great attentiveness: that in regard to himself our Lord God cannot forgive, for he cannot be angry—it would be an impossibility. For this is what was shown: that our life is all grounded and rooted in love, and without love we cannot live; and therefore to the soul which through God's special grace sees so much of his great and marvelous goodness, and sees that we are joined to him in love for ever, it is the greatest impossibility conceivable that God should be angry, for anger and friendship are two contraries.[68]

LT 49, P. 112

69 God secretly and steadily works to draw us toward mercy and grace, always seeking to bring us life and love. For that reason we need to be honest with ourselves, recognizing the ways we act to dishonor the image and likeness of God in one another. As we focus on our own propensity to hurt others and to thwart the divine love in all things and in all places, we do realize our need for forgiveness. It can be deeply sobering to emerge from our spiritual fog and clearly see the ways in which we have forgotten that we are always in God. Deep within us, God is working toward the peace that passes all understanding.

I saw quite clearly that where our Lord appears, everything is peaceful and there is no place for anger; for I saw no kind of anger in God, neither for a short time nor for a long one; indeed, it seems to me that if God could be even slightly angry we could never have any life or place or being; for as truly as we have our being from the eternal strength of God and from the eternal wisdom and from the eternal goodness, so truly are we sustained in the eternal strength of God, in the eternal wisdom and in the eternal goodness; though we feel vengeful, quarrelsome and contentious, yet we are all mercifully enclosed in the kindness of God and in his gentleness, in his generosity and in his indulgence; for I saw quite certainly that our eternal support, our dwelling, our life and our being are all in God; for as his endless goodness protects us when we sin so that we do not perish, the same endless goodness continually negotiates a peace in us in place of our anger and our contentious falling, and makes us see that what is needed is that with true fear we should heartily beseech God for forgiveness with a gracious longing for our salvation; for we cannot be blessedly saved until we are truly in a state of peace and love, for that is what our salvation means.[69]

LT 49, P. 112

1 Julian's showings begin when she is close to death, and on her sick-bed looks on the crucifix held out to her by her priest. As she gazes at the figure of the crucified Jesus, suddenly, without her asking for them, the visions begin. She sees Jesus crucified and vividly captures what she sees. Her vision echoes the vivid devotional art of her time, where Christ's sufferings become the object of meditation as the believer enters into them fully. Julian's description is intensely physical, noticing changes due to blood loss, to rigor prior to death, to the weight of the body hanging from nails.

2 Julian appears to understand the crucifixion as a onetime historical event that also reveals eternal truth. She doesn't believe that Jesus is suffering a second time. Rather, in this moment of revelation, her finely tuned intuition brings her to the place of the cross as she receives the gift of divine instruction so that she may know well the truth of this love.

4 □ Christ's Passion

The blessed body was abandoned and drying for a long
time, becoming distorted because of the nails and its own
weight; for I understood that because the dear hands and
the dear feet were so tender, the great size, hardness and
grievousness of the nails made the wounds become wider,
and the body sagged with its own weight from hanging for
such a long time.[1]

LT 17, PP. 65–66

This showing of Christ's pain filled me with pain, though
I knew well he only suffered once, yet he wanted to show
it to me and fill me with awareness of it as I had wished
previously.[2]

LT 17, P. 67

3 When Julian gazes at this vision of the crucified Christ, she feels he is telling her that we are united to him in pain. The moments of his Passion and death are a divine show-and-tell in which God reveals that no creaturely pain is foreign to Jesus. On the cross, once and for all, God in Christ makes the depths of love known.

4 From the time of the early church, Christians believed that when Christ died, the whole creation grieved. This follows from the New Testament account that at the moment of Jesus's death, the earth shook and rocks were split apart. The death of Jesus is pictured as a cosmic event revealing that Jesus is the Christ, the Son of God, and on the cross takes on the ultimate separation and isolation of body, mind, and spirit (see Matthew 27:50–53).

5 The natural world, knowing God to be its creator, recognized God in Christ on the cross. Then the firmament and the earth grieved in solidarity with the pain endured by the Divine, on behalf of the whole of the universe. Because every speck of matter is in Christ in whom "all things hold together" (Colossians 1:17), all matter is stunned by the depths of love.

6 Jesus is not solely in heaven; Jesus is Julian's heaven. Jesus becomes an eternal place, a home for which we are ever intended and in whom we live. Choosing Jesus as heaven, in good times and bad, means remembering that we are grounded and rooted in divine love at all times and in all places. When Julian chooses Jesus as heaven, she chooses to be open solely to God's perspective and let go of her own best-loved notions and interpretations.

7 For Julian, the historical events of Jesus's birth, life, suffering, death, and resurrection reveal eternal truth. Yes, Jesus was crucified at a particular time and place to show the truth of God's participation in our suffering and pain. Yet Julian does not believe that God is in the business of creating suffering; rather, God is *in* our suffering, enduring the worst that humanity has to offer and transforming it.

Here I saw a great union between Christ and us, as I understand it; for when he was in pain, we were in pain. And all
creatures who were capable of suffering, suffered with him,
that is to say, all the creatures that God has made to serve
us.[3] At the time of Christ's dying, the firmament and the
earth failed for sorrow, each according to their nature.[4] For
it is their natural property to recognize as their God him in
whom all their natural power is grounded; when he failed
then by their very natures they had as far as possible to fail
with him from sorrow at his pain.[5]

LT 18, P. 68

Thus I was taught to choose Jesus as my heaven, though
at that time I saw him only in pain. I was satisfied by no
heaven but Jesus, who will be my bliss when I go there. And
it has always been a comfort to me that I chose Jesus for
my heaven, through his grace, in all this time of suffering
and sorrow. And that has been a lesson to me, that I should
do so for evermore, choosing Jesus alone for my heaven in
good and bad times.[6]

LT 19, P. 69

For as long as he was capable of suffering, he felt pain and
sorrow for us; and now that he has ascended into heaven
and is beyond human pain, he is still suffering with us.[7]

LT 20, P. 71

8 | It was commonly thought that Jesus's death on the cross was a sacrifice offered by God the Father to appease divine wrath toward sinners. Julian, a laywoman and an anchoress, sees the deep theological flaw in this teaching. She comes to understand the extravagance of divine love.

9 | As she beholds the suffering of Christ on the cross, Julian proclaims that God is present in all suffering, including our own. This is the meaning of "we are now, as our Lord intends it, dying with him on his cross in our pain and our passion." For contrary to our present-day assumption that a good life is life with no pain, Julian would say that pain may be the way in which we are awakened to our true ground and origin, and through which we remember our common humanity and friendship with one another in God.

And I, contemplating all this through his grace, saw that his love for our souls is so strong that he chose the pain willingly and eagerly, and suffered it meekly and was well-pleased to do so; for the souls who contemplate it in this way, when touched by grace, shall truly see that the pain of Christ's Passion surpasses all pain: that is to say, it surpasses the pains which will be turned into supreme and everlasting joys by virtue of Christ's Passion.[8]

LT 20, P. 71

I understood that we are now, as our Lord intends it, dying with him on his cross in our pain and our passion; and if we willingly remain on the same cross with his help and his grace until the final moment, the countenance he turns on us will suddenly change, and we shall be with him in heaven. There will be no time between one moment and the next, and everything will be turned to joy; and this is what he meant in this showing: "Where is there now one jot of your pain or your sorrow?" And we shall be entirely blessed.[9]

LT 21, PP. 71–72

10 Here Julian portrays Jesus speaking to her directly. In this radical proclamation, Jesus assures Julian that he offers his suffering purely out of love. His tender and abundant care leads him to assure her that if needed, he would have suffered even more.

11 How might humanity be Jesus's "crown"? On the one hand, this statement reveals the royal dimension of our human nature; we are invited into Christ's reign. It also reminds us that unlike a political kingdom, the kingdom of Christ is characterized by loving care, the sharing of one another's burdens, and a radical willingness to encounter evil with vulnerability.

12 Perhaps as a parent, a sibling, or a friend, you have known that desire to suffer on behalf of another, or even to die in another's place. The fullness of divine love shown in Jesus also knows no bounds, but is willing to endure death so that we may truly live.

Then our good Lord Jesus Christ spoke, asking, "Are you
well pleased that I suffered for you?" I said, "Yes, my good
Lord, thank you. Yes, my good Lord, blessed may you be!"
Then Jesus, our kind Lord, said, "If you are pleased, I am
pleased. It is a joy, a delight and an endless happiness to me
that I ever endured suffering for you, and if I could suffer
more, I would suffer more."[10]

LT 22, P. 73

We are his joy, we are his reward, we are his glory, we are
his crown—and this was a special marvel and a thrilling
vision, that we should be his crown.[11]

LT 22, P. 73

Then his meaning is this: "How should I not do all that
I can for love of you?—for doing so does not grieve me,
since I would die for love of you so often with no concern
for my bitter pain."[12]

LT 22, P. 73

13 On the cross, God is revealed in Jesus to be the glad giver, one who gives without stint, without counting the cost, for the sheer joy of it. In our own lives, we may glimpse sacrificial giving in one another, but hardly ever sustain it throughout a lifetime. This is the generosity that is at the heart of divine love, and in whose image we are made.

14 During the crucifixion Jesus's side was pierced by a sword (John 19:34), and water and blood came forth. Here Julian echoes the story of Jesus's post-resurrection appearance to his disciples, when Thomas, the doubter, will only believe if he can see and touch the wound. The risen Christ says to him, "Reach out your hand and put it in my side" (John 20:27). Julian takes this even further—the wound in Jesus's side is so spacious that all may rest there, at peace. This love holds all that has been made, and all that has been made dwells *within* that love. This beautiful "wound" is the place where the whole cosmos resides.

And with these words he brought to mind the nature of a glad giver: a glad giver pays little attention to the thing he is giving, but his whole desire and intention is to please and comfort the one to whom he gives it; and if the receiver values the gift highly and takes it gratefully, then the generous giver thinks nothing of all his hardship and the price he had to pay, because of the joy and delight that he feels at having pleased and comforted the one he loves. This was shown abundantly and fully.[13]

LT 23, P. 75

Then, with a glad face, our Lord looked into his side, and gazed, rejoicing; and with his dear gaze he led his creature's understanding through the same wound into his side. And then he revealed a beautiful and delightful place which was large enough for all mankind who shall be saved to rest there in peace and love.[14]

LT 24, P. 76

15 Julian trusts that the Lord is joy incarnate. From the cross Jesus assures her that his passage from life through death to risen life, though arduous and terribly painful, was a passage offered freely, out of abundant love.

16 The phrase "It is I" echoes the voice from the burning bush to Moses in Exodus: "I am who I am" (3:14). This mysterious Hebrew phrase is almost untranslatable. The repeated use of "I" also echoes Jesus's "I am" sayings from the Gospel of John, such as "I am the light of the world" (John 8:12).

17 Julian perceives that through the act of compassion we are able to dwell in Christ, and he in us. This union is strengthened each time we cooperate with the Spirit who is known in mercy, kindness, and compassion.

These blessed words were said: "Look how I loved you.
Look and see that I loved you so much before I died for you
that I was willing to die for you; and now I have died for
you, and willingly suffered as much as I can for you. And
now all my bitter torment and painful hardship has changed
into endless joy and bliss for me and for you. How could it
now be that you could make any request that pleased me
that I would not very gladly grant you? For my pleasure is
your holiness and your endless joy and bliss with me."[15]

LT 24, P. 76

Our Lord Jesus said repeatedly, "It is I, it is I; it is I who am
highest; it is I you love; it is I who delight you; it is I you
serve; it is I you long for; it is I you desire; it is I who am your
purpose; it is I who am all; it is I that Holy Church preaches
and teaches you; it is I who showed myself to you here."[16]

LT 26, P. 78

And then I saw that whenever a man feels kind compassion
with love for his fellow Christian, it is Christ within him.[17]

LT 28, P. 81

18 Here Julian makes a connection between Christ's humiliation on the cross and the fruit that comes forth from his humiliation, which is compassion. This is the compassion that Christ bestows on us in order to draw us more closely into his life. Because Christ is so deeply involved with us, he abides with us in any pain and suffering we endure, eventually healing and making us new.

19 Julian leads us to see that the Passion and death of Jesus show us how God longs for us. In Jesus Christ, God reveals this divine yearning, an eternal "love-longing." That is the essence of divine love.

20 Julian teaches that just as God longs for us, so we long for God. This mutual longing is sacred and holy.

That same humiliation which was revealed in his Passion was revealed again here in this compassion, in which there were two ways of understanding our Lord's meaning: one was the bliss to which we are brought and in which he will rejoice, the other is for strength in our suffering; for he wants us to know that it will all be turned into glory and profit by virtue of his Passion, and to know we do not suffer alone, but with him, recognizing that we are grounded in him, and he wants us to see that his pain and his humiliation go so far beyond all that we may suffer that it cannot be fully conceived.[18]

LT 28, P. 81

For some of us that shall be saved, and shall be Christ's joy and his bliss, are still here on earth, and some are yet to come, and it shall be so until that last day. Therefore it seems to me that this is his thirst: a love-longing to have us all together, wholly in himself for his delight; for we are not now as wholly in him as we shall be then.[19]

LT 31, P. 83

For as truly as there is a property of compassion and pity in God, so there is as truly a property of thirst and longing in God. And because of the strength of this longing in Christ it is for us in turn to long for him, and without this no soul comes to heaven.[20]

LT 31, P. 84

21 Jesus, with the compassion of a mother, graciously chooses to endure the Passion suffering for our sake—"as though the soul had been in pain and in prison." He reassures us that there is only joy awaiting us. Julian sees the Lord as joyous and pleased.

22 Sure and steady in her received perceptions and the years of prayer and reflection, Julian knows that "all manner of things" are prepared by the God who loves us. When we awaken to this reality we can be secure in our trust in God, even when our lives seem to shatter. All is held in the hand of God, as the hazelnut was held in Julian's hand.

23 As Julian meditated on her showings, she also came to reflect deeply on time itself. She sees that in the moment of death on the cross, the man Jesus did suffer and die. This knowledge gave her, she says, "three kinds of understanding of the expression of our Lord's face," human and divine. The "first face" is truly a face of pain and death, yet it is also "cheerful," for this is God in Christ, whose love for us has led to this offering. The second face reveals the pity and grief with which God sees our sorrows and hardships. And lastly, she sees the "blessed face," the eternal face of true joy and compassion.

And then our kind Lord reveals himself, very joyfully and looking very pleased, with a friendly welcome, as though the soul had been in pain and in prison, sweetly saying this: "My darling, I am glad you have come to me. I have always been with you in all your misery and now you can see how much I love you and we are united in bliss." This is how sins are forgiven through mercy and grace and our souls gloriously received in joy, just as they will be when they come to heaven, whenever this occurs through the gracious working of the Holy Ghost and the power of Christ's Passion.[21]

LT 40, p. 97

Here I really understood that all manner of things are made ready for us by the great goodness of God, so much so that when we are ourselves in a state of peace and love we are truly safe.[22]

LT 40, p. 97

I have three kinds of understanding of the expression of our Lord's face. The first is the suffering face which he showed while he was here, dying. Although this is a sight of mourning and sorrow, it is also glad and cheerful, for he is God. The second face is pity, grief and compassion; and he shows this face to all those who love him, with the certainty of protection for those who need his mercy. The third is the blessed face which he will show for ever, and I saw this oftenest and longest.[23]

LT 71, p. 158

1 | Julian firmly holds to trinitarian doctrine, discerning that each person of the Trinity—Father, Son, and Holy Spirit—fully indwells the others in love; they are distinct, but not separate. Not only was this the orthodox teaching of the church, but also the true nature of what she received from her visions. All of the love of God is mirrored in the Passion of Christ on the cross. Note that Julian does not interpret the Passion as the Father acting upon the Son, as some medieval theologians taught. One person of the Trinity cannot act against another. That would fracture the communion of divine love.

5 □ The Trinity

The whole Trinity took part in the Passion of Christ, dispensing an abundance of virtues and fullness of grace to us through him, but only the Son of the Virgin suffered; and because of this the whole blessed Trinity is eternally joyful. And this was shown in these words, "Are you well pleased?" and by Christ's other words, "If you are pleased, I am pleased," as if he said, "It is joy and delight enough to me, and I ask nothing more of you for my hardship but that I give you pleasure."[1]

LT 23, P. 75

2 God's love for humankind came even before the creation of the world. There was never a time when this was not the truth.

3 From the beginning, the Trinity has been awaiting the full revelation of love and mercy in Christ. In the crucifixion of Jesus, humankind was given a historical event that reveals eternal truth: the love of God, beyond measure and beyond words, embracing and enfolding human life from birth to death, and gathering all created life fully into divine being.

4 Human nature is essentially divine. Our souls are of God's own essence, so we can never be completely separated from divine love. If separation were to truly happen, we would cease to exist. Even when we are at our worst, we are still in God.

5 Julian sees that our origin is in God, even though we are *not* God. She does not confuse humanity with divinity; humanity comes forth from the love of the Trinity. It is like the love of a father, a mother. That love is the womb from which we spring.

I saw that God never began to love humankind, for just as
humankind shall be in eternal bliss, completing the joy of
God in his own works, so has that same humankind been,
in God's foresight, known and loved according to God's
righteous purpose since before time began.[2] And by the
eternal consent and agreement of the whole Trinity, Christ
would be the ground and the head of these fair beings, he
from whom we all come, in whom we are all enclosed, into
whom we shall return; finding in him our full heaven of
everlasting joy through the foreseeing purpose of the whole
blessed Trinity since before time began.[3] Before he made us
he loved us, and when we were made we loved him; and this
is a love made of the essential goodness natural to the Holy
Ghost, mighty by reason of the might of the Father, and
wise in accordance with the wisdom of the Son. Thus man's
soul is made of God and bound to God by the same ties.[4]

LT 53, PP. 128–129

And I saw no difference between God and our essential
being, it seemed to be all God, and yet my understanding
took it that our essential being is in God: that is to say that
God is God, and our essential being is a creation within
God; for the almighty truth of the Trinity is our father,
he who made us and keeps us within him; and the deep
wisdom of the Trinity is our mother, in whom we are all
enclosed; and the great goodness of the Trinity is our Lord
and in him we are enclosed and he in us.[5]

LT 54, P. 130

6 God, who is Trinity, is also the source of loving relationship. In that relationship we are made whole and complete. Divine love heals us, restores us, and receives us.

7 In our creation, the Trinity brings forth our souls from the divine life. Our bodily life—in Julian's phrase, our "lower nature"—is loved and revealed to be sacred through Jesus's embodiment. In Jesus, God who is Trinity inhabits our bodies, knowing their wonders and limitations from the inside out.

8 According to Christian thought and faith, the Trinity of Father, Son, and Holy Spirit acts in a single, unified way. Just as in Christ divinity and humanity are united, so in Christ our lower and higher natures are knit together so that body and soul are one. The "higher nature" (soul) is hidden with Christ, essentially mysterious to us, and never dies.

9 Julian maintains that "liking and love" is the quality of the Trinity in which we should put our trust above all. She refers to the "delight" and "pleasure" God takes in humankind, a love that is gentle beyond description and kind beyond our imagining. Moreover, when we begin to recognize and trust in this love, we are less prey to depression and doubt.

I saw that our nature is complete in God, and he makes diverse qualities flow into it from him to do his will, and these are sustained by nature, and restored and completed by mercy and grace.[6] And none of these shall be lost; for the higher part of our nature is bound to God in its creation; and God is bound to the lower part of our nature in taking on our flesh.[7] Thus the two parts of us are united in Christ; for the Trinity is included in Christ in whom the highest part of our nature is grounded and rooted, and the second Person of the Trinity has taken on the lower part, a nature which was ordained for him from the beginning; for I saw quite certainly that all the works which God had done or ever shall do were fully known to him and foreseen since before time began; and he made mankind for love, and for the same love chose to be man himself.[8]

LT 57, P. 135

For of all the properties of the Holy Trinity, it is God's wish that we should place most reliance and take most delight in liking and love; for love makes God's power and wisdom very gentle to us; for just as through his generosity God forgives our sin when we repent, so he wants us to forget our sin of unreasonable depression and doubtful fear.[9]

LT 73, P. 162

1 For Julian, sin gets in the way of our relationship with God and with one another; sin keeps us from him. Sin is an obstacle to living the goodness of God.

2 Julian forthrightly asks: Why does God allow sin to exist? Would not it have been better to create a world in which sin and evil were not possibilities?

3 Julian revisits this question again and again. Why does sin exist? How can its presence be part of a cosmos created out of love?

4 The Lord answers Julian's question by saying, "Sin is befitting." In the original Middle English, the phrase is "sin is behovely." (Our modern English word "behoove" gives us the sense of "behovely," meaning "suitable" or "right.") In other words, sin has a function—it is, in some way, necessary. Yet Jesus follows this with a further affirmation: "All shall be well." Sin is never the last word.

6 □ The Question of Sin

After this, our Lord reminded me of the longing I had had
for him; and I saw that nothing kept me from him but sin,
and I saw that this is so with all of us.[1] And I thought that
if sin had never existed, we should have been pure and
like himself, as God made us, and so I had often wondered
before now in my folly why, in his great foreseeing wisdom, God had not prevented the beginning of sin; for then,
I thought, all would have been well.[2] I ought certainly to
have abandoned these thoughts, but nevertheless I grieved
and sorrowed over the question with no reason or judgment.[3] But Jesus, who in this vision informed me of all that I
needed to know, answered with this assurance: "Sin is befitting, but all shall be well, and all shall be well, and all manner of things shall be well."[4]

LT 27, P. 79

5 For Julian, the word "sin" sums up the whole of human violence, from the personal to the political. It refers to all the ways in which we do not honor and respect one another, the creation, and God. But on the cross, in some ultimately mysterious way, Jesus took all of that sin upon himself. By refusing to answer violence with anything but love, he revealed to us the way that leads to life. And he gave us a promise: death and violence will not triumph.

6 Following in the teaching of Augustine of Hippo, Julian sees that sin is parasitic—it cannot exist in and of itself, but is a distortion of all that is good. Because evil cannot come from a good God, it cannot exist in and of itself. Instead evil is a vacuum, an absence of love, and for Julian sin itself "has no sort of substance." It can only be seen in its painful and destructive results.

7 The suffering sin brings does lead us to pray for mercy. Perhaps we have participated directly in sinful patterns of behavior ourselves; perhaps we have been injured by or even benefited from the sins of someone else. In either case, sin brings us face to face with our need of God.

With this bare word "sin" our Lord brought to my mind the
whole extent of all that is not good, and the shameful scorn
and the utter humiliation that he bore for us in this life, and
his dying, and all the pains and sufferings of all his creatures, both in body and spirit—for we are all to some extent
brought to nothing and shall be brought to nothing as our
master Jesus was, until we are fully purged: that is to say
until our mortal flesh is brought completely to nothing, and
all those of our inward feelings which are not truly good.
He gave me insight into these things, along with all pains
that ever were and ever shall be; and compared with these I
realize that Christ's Passion was the greatest pain and went
beyond them all.[5]

LT 27, P. 79

But I did not see sin; for I believe it has no sort of substance
nor portion of being, nor could it be recognized were it not
for the suffering it causes.[6] And this suffering seems to me to
be something transient, for it purges us and makes us know
ourselves and pray for mercy; for the Passion of our Lord
supports us against all this, and that is his blessed will.[7]

LT 27, PP. 79–80

8 Just as Julian sees that there is no anger in God, so she also sees that God does not blame us for sin. She seems to say that if sin is of so little consequence to God, we should not allow it to obscure the true reality of God's mercy and compassion. Our task is to discover that love, know that love with our whole being, and seek to align our lives to the requirements of that eternal yearning and delight. We also need to perceive that sin is a distortion of the communion of love for which we are intended. Divine love transcends sin and will make all well.

9 As Julian reflects on the effects of sin on her fellow humans, it deepens her sense of compassion. She is not led to judgment, but to mercy. Her sense that we all are shaken like "a cloth in the wind" by the effects of sin helps her to perceive human fragility in the face of this force. Julian will not avert her gaze from the truth—life is good and beautiful, and it is fraught with violence, illness, war, and deprivation. She brings all of this awareness into her contemplative reflection. Divine love, though not the cause of sin, will create something great from it.

10 Julian does not see sin. It is, from her theological perspective, without true substance, although this does not mean it has no effect. It means that sin has no reality in and of itself. It is a perversion of love, and we know it by the pain and suffering that result from it.

11 The suffering caused by sin is both real and transitory. From the eternal perspective, sin's effects have no lasting effect, for divine love will heal and restore all that sin has wrecked.

"It is true that sin is the cause of all this suffering, but all shall be well, and all shall be well, and all manner of things shall be well." These words were said very tenderly, with no suggestion that I or anyone who will be saved was being blamed. It would therefore be very strange to blame or wonder at God because of my sin, since he does not blame me for sinning.[8]

LT 27, P. 80

Thus I saw how Christ feels compassion for us because of sin. And just as I was earlier filled with suffering and compassion at the Passion of Christ, so was I now also partly filled with compassion for all my fellow Christians, for those well-beloved people who shall be saved; that is to say, God's servants, Holy Church, will be shaken in sorrows and anguish and tribulation in this world, as men shake a cloth in the wind. And God answered as follows: "I shall make some great thing out of this in heaven, something eternally worthy and everlastingly joyful."[9]

LT 28, P. 80

But I did not see sin; for I believe it has no sort of substance nor portion of being, nor could it be recognized were it not for the suffering it causes.[10] And this suffering seems to me to be something transient, for it purges us and makes us know ourselves and pray for mercy; for the Passion of our Lord supports us against all this, and that is his blessed will.[11]

LT 27, PP. 79–80

12 As is the case with any revelation, something is illuminated and something remains hidden. In this case, a great mystery surrounds *how* all shall be made well. When Julian presses for an explanation, wondering how this might be, she discerns a great mystery hidden in God. Her theological reflection tells her that, as a finite creature, she can never fully comprehend who God is nor the specifics of how God will make all things well.

13 Julian recognizes that we can make ourselves miserable by failing to trust in God. This is not a facile explanation, but one arrived at after years of reflection, prayer, and questioning of her own showings. She has been honest and faithful in interrogating the revelations given to her. She has also discovered that there is a limit to what the human mind and soul can understand. Following Paul, she observes that some things are "hidden with Christ" (Colossians 3:3), and she is willing to let herself accept that.

14 The famous phrase "all shall be well" comes from this passage in which the Lord responds to her pressing questions about the role of sin in our lives and in our relationship to God and our neighbor. "All shall be well" is an eschatological statement intended to evoke hope in ultimate reality and in the working of divine providence. That is why it is not facile or easy. Julian hopes in God because she has been given unshakable confidence in divine compassion.

15 God shows Julian that sin is intrinsic to our human condition. Each and every person bears this affliction, and each and every person is welcome to receive the healing mercy of love.

And in these same words I saw a marvelous great mystery hidden in God, a mystery which he will make openly known to us in heaven, in which knowledge we shall truly see the reason why he allowed sin to exist; and seeing this we shall rejoice eternally in our Lord God.[12]

LT 27, P. 80

It is proper for his servant, out of obedience and reverence, not to know his counsel too well. Our Lord feels pity and compassion for us because some people are so anxious to know about it; and I am sure that if we knew how much we would please him and set our own minds at rest by leaving the matter alone, then we would do so.[13]

LT 30, P. 82

And thus our good Lord answered all the questions and doubts I could put forward, saying most comfortingly, "I may make all things well, I can make all things well and I will make all things well and I shall make all things well; and you shall see for yourself that all manner of things shall be well."[14]

LT 31, P. 83

God reminded me that I would sin; and because of my pleasure in contemplating him, I was slow to pay attention to that showing. And our Lord very kindly waited and gave me the grace to pay attention.[15]

LT 37, P. 93

16 Sin may also be a way that we awaken to our need for relationship with God, and realize that we need the medicine of divine mercy. Seeing our sins clearly may startle us into discovering that God is always with us, indwelling our souls and bodies, and healing us from the inside out.

17 Julian notices that when we find ourselves feeling lost and griefstricken due to sin, God is immediately there to heal and make us new. She is not saying that God is the source of sin, nor that God tests us to see if we will fall. She is saying that sin, as a distortion of divine life and love, has a real effect on how we live. When circumstances force us to see this, even though we are shaken by the discovery, we can be sure of God's tender willingness to offer mercy and compassion. She does not sense that we encounter wrath or severity from God, but rather everlasting aid and kindness.

18 Whatever wounds we may bear because of sin are witnesses to divine love and healing. Wounded we may be—yet wounds are occasions for us to rejoice in God's own kindness and to remember that "all shall be well."

God also showed that sin shall not be shameful to man, but his glory; for in the same way as God's justice gives every sin a suitable punishment, so God's love gives the same soul a joy for every sin.[16]

LT 38, P. 94

Our Lord takes tender care of us when we feel that we are almost forsaken and cast away because of our sin and because we have deserved it. And because of the humility which we gain through this, we are raised by God's grace right up high in his sight, with great contrition, with compassion and with a true longing for God. Then we are immediately freed from sin and suffering and taken up into bliss and even made exalted saints. By contrition we are made pure, by compassion we are made ready and by true longing for God we are made worthy.[17]

LT 39, PP. 95–96

Although a man has the scars of healed wounds, when he appears before God they do not deface but ennoble him.[18]

LT 39, P. 96

19 Julian tells us that sin is never bigger than God. Because of God's infinite mercy and love, sin cannot ever have the final word on our lives. No matter how deeply enmeshed we may be in sinful behaviors, the grace and mercy of God are ever present for healing and wholeness. God's "naked hatred" for sin (and only for sin) may come alive in us, leading us to rightly know sin for what it is, and to see its destructive power in ourselves and in others.

20 Our stubborn lack of perception keeps us from seeing the divine presence within ourselves and one another. We forget that true perception and clear-sightedness are basically subjective, so that who we are and how we see shapes *what* we see.

21 Julian acknowledges the hard struggle of a life of faith. We catch momentary glimpses of divine love and just as quickly lose sight of it again. Julian senses God's presence and knows theoretically that this presence works love within us.

Just as his love for us does not fail because of our sin,
he does not want our love for ourselves and our fellow
Christians to fail; we must feel naked hatred for sin and
unending love for the soul, as God loves it. Then we shall
hate sin as God hates it and love the soul as God loves it;
for this assertion of God's is an endless help and comfort: "I
am keeping you very safe."[19]

LT 40, P. 98

I understood that we men are changeable in this life and
through frailty and accident we fall into sin. Man is naturally weak and foolish, and his will is smothered; and in this
world he suffers storm and sorrow and woe, and the cause is
his own blindness—he does not see God; for if he saw God
continually he would have no evil feelings, nor any sort of
impulse towards the craving which leads to sin.[20]

LT 47, P. 109

And yet in this I saw from God's showing that this kind of
sight of him cannot continue in this life—cannot for his own
glory and the augmentation of our endless joy. And therefore we often lack the sight of him, and we are immediately
thrown back into ourselves, where we find no right feelings,
nothing but our own contrariness, and that of the ancient
root of our first sin with all those contrived by ourselves that
follow from it; and in this we are tossed and troubled with all
the many different feelings of sin and suffering, both of the
body and the soul, which are known to us in this life.[21]

LT 47, P. 110

22 God pities us because one of the cruelest effects of sin is that it keeps us from seeing "our Lord's blessed face." We allow ourselves to become captive to our own distorted perceptions. This is a kind of death, for we cannot gaze upon the face of divine love.

23 The love-longing that characterizes God's relationship with us is never-ending. While our sins may continue to weigh us down in every way, that will not last forever. Nothing can come between us and the bliss that God intends for us. Here Julian again sounds like Paul: "For I am convinced that neither death, nor life, nor angels, nor rulers, nor things present, nor things to come, nor powers, nor height, nor depth, nor anything else in all creation, will be able to separate us from the love of God in Christ Jesus our Lord" (Romans 8:38–39).

24 Because God is beyond human comprehension, Julian admits she cannot know fully how the conundrum of sin will be resolved. Much as she would like to know fully how "all will be made well," her visions have taught her that there is a great mystery hidden in God. Julian comes to accept that it is beyond our human faculties to understand fully the role of sin.

And so our Lord's blessed face was shown with an expression of pity, and in this showing I saw that sin is diametri-
cally opposed to it, to such an extent that as long as we are
mingled with any portion of sin, we shall never clearly see
our Lord's blessed face. And the more horrible and grievous
our sins are, the more deeply we are sunk below this blessed
sight at that moment. And therefore it often seems to us as
if we are in peril of death, and partly in hell, because of the
pain and sorrow which sin causes us. And so we are dead
for the time being to the true sight of our blessed life.[22] But
in all this I certainly saw that we are not dead in the sight
of God, nor does he ever leave us; but he will never have
his full bliss in us until we have our full bliss in him, truly
seeing his fair, blessed face; this is ordained for us by nature
and obtained by us through grace. So I saw how mortal sin
exists for a short time in the blessed beings that will gain
everlasting life.[23]

LT 72, PP. 159–160

And in these same words I saw a marvelous great mystery hidden in God, a mystery which he will make openly
known to us in heaven, in which knowledge we shall truly
see the reason why he allowed sin to exist; and seeing this
we shall rejoice eternally in our Lord God.[24]

LT 27, P. 80

25 God, who is concerned with simple and humble things as well as great, and is infinitely aware of the whole created order, beholds each point in time and space, even the smallest. In this way Julian coaxes us to imagine our way into the divine perspective, which is outside of time and infinite. As Jesus says, "Even the hairs of your head are all counted" (Matthew 10:30).

26 In struggling to understand God's promise that all will be well, Julian must not flinch from the pains and difficulties that have been visited on her time. She has experienced the reality of households being wiped out by plague, widespread privation and want, soldiers returning from war both wounded and embittered. When she hears "all shall be well," she holds that in tension with the realities around her. The notion that "all shall be well" is not a placebo, but a profound summing up of the power of divine love to enfold the worst that we may suffer.

27 For the medieval church, "the last day" referred to a day of wrath and judgment, the end of time, when God would consign the souls of the sinful and unrepentant to eternal damnation. Julian's theology, however, does not share this view. Instead, she sees the last day as the time at which God's way of love is fully revealed, and all shall see fully what is hidden with Christ.

On the one hand he wants us to know that he does not only concern himself with great and noble things, but also with small, humble and simple things, with both one and the other; this is what he means when he says, "All manner of things shall be well"; for he wants us to know that the smallest thing shall not be forgotten.[25]

LT 32, P. 85

But another thing understood is this: deeds are done which appear so evil to us and people suffer such terrible evils that it does not seem as though any good will ever come of them; and we consider this, sorrowing and grieving over it so that we cannot find peace in the blessed contemplation of God as we should do; and this is why: our reasoning powers are so blind now, so humble and so simple, that we cannot know the high, marvelous wisdom, the might and the goodness of the Holy Trinity. And this is what he means when he says, "You shall see for yourself that all manner of things shall be well," as if he said, "Pay attention to this now, faithfully and confidently, and at the end of time you will truly see it in the fullness of joy."[26]

LT 32, P. 85

It appears to me that there is a deed which the Holy Trinity shall do on the last day, and when that deed shall be done and how it shall be done is unknown to all creatures under Christ, and shall be until it has been done.[27]

LT 32, P. 85

28 This mysterious great deed, beyond our understanding or perception, is truly of God. Therefore, God teaches her, we cannot penetrate its mystery. The Lord tells Julian that what seems utterly impossible to her is, from the divine perspective, indeed possible. Because of that, all shall be well. Again, we are led to consider the possibility that the human viewpoint is always limited, finite, and conditioned by social location, circumstance, history, and culture.

And given all this, I thought it impossible that all manner
of things should be well, as our Lord revealed at this time.
And I received no other answer in showing from our Lord
God but this: "What is impossible to you is not impossible
to me. I shall keep my word in all things and I shall make all
things well."[28]

LT 32, P. 86

1 Prayer is essentially relationship with God, a relationship of love, mutual giving, and delight. "God of your goodness, give me yourself," Julian prays. She is able to ask this in full confidence that God is good beyond our imagining, love beyond our desiring, and hope beyond our dreaming.

2 Julian counsels us to pray for an ever-deepening relationship with this God of love. To pray only for what we might want from God, rather than to be *with* God, leads to a shallow relationship. It is analogous to relationships in which we value people only because of what they can provide for us—money, security, status, reassurance—rather than because we love them for themselves.

3 Aligning our desires with God's desires is the ongoing task of prayer. Julian recognizes that because we are not God and do not have God's insight, there are aspects of divine mystery we will never understand. And that is as it should be. Julian's reflections in this passage are reminiscent of the words of the prophet Isaiah: "For my thoughts are not your thoughts, nor are your ways my ways, says the Lord. For as the heavens are higher than the earth, so are my ways higher than your ways and my thoughts than your thoughts" (Isaiah 55:8–9).

7 □ Prayer and Faith

For, as I understand this showing, it is the natural yearning of the soul touched by the Holy Ghost to say, "God, of your goodness, give me yourself; you are enough for me, and anything less that I could ask for would not do you full honor.[1] And if I ask anything that is less, I shall always lack something, but in you alone I have everything."[2]

LT 5, P. 48

And we must pray to be like our brothers and sisters who are saints in heaven and who only want what God wants, then all our joy will be in God and we shall be content both with what is hidden and with what is shown; for I saw our Lord's purpose quite clearly: the more anxious we are to discover his secret knowledge about this or anything else, the further we shall be from knowing it.[3]

LT 33, P. 88

4 Well practiced in prayer, Julian knows the reality of those times of aridity, when we are "barren and dry," and God seems completely absent. She knows that the life of prayer is not always easy, nor will it invariably comfort and console us.

5 In this passage God speaks directly to Julian, reminding her that all desire, including the desire for prayer, has a single source. God is the wellspring of our prayer, moving within us, awakening the desire to pray. Because God has stirred the desire, it will be fulfilled, in God's time.

6 Julian assures us that prayer, initiated by God's own Spirit acting within us, unites us to God. She uses the language of betrothal; through prayer we are "fast-bound," which refers to handfasting. The hands of those desiring to marry were bound together with ribbon or cloth to signify their unity in marriage.

7 Our prayers are received with joy by the Lord. Julian urges the reader to pray with the confidence that prayers return to the God who initiated the desire to pray. The prayers are of God, with God, in God, and our prayer is treasured by God.

8 Prayers have a spiritual presence of their own, dwelling with the community of saints in eternity. Prayer, that goodness that is of God, is life and light.

But yet often we do not trust him fully for it seems to us
that because of our unworthiness, and because we are feeling absolutely nothing, we cannot be certain that God is
hearing our prayers. For often we are as barren and dry after
our prayers as we were before, and so we feel our folly is
the cause of our weakness; I have felt like this myself.[4]

LT 41, P. 99

"I am the foundation of your prayers: first it is my will that
you should have something, and then I make you desire it,
and then I make you pray for it; and if you pray for it, then
how could it be that you should not have what you pray for?"[5]

LT 41, P. 99

Prayer is a new, gracious, lasting will of the soul united and
fast-bound to the will of God by the precious and mysterious working of the Holy Ghost.[6] Our Lord, he is the chief
receiver of our prayers, it seems to me, and he accepts them
very gratefully and with much delight; and he sends them
up above and puts them in a treasury where they will never
perish.[7] They are there in the presence of God and all his
holy ones, being received continually, always helping us in
our need, and when we finally receive our bliss they will be
given to us as a stage in our joy, with endless and glorious
thanks from God.[8]

LT 41, PP. 99–100

9 Speaking directly to her, the Lord assures Julian that even when prayer seems utterly fruitless and unproductive, it still brings joy and delight to God. Persevering in prayer is a way of persevering in relationship, growing in love and trust even when it brings no feelings of warmth, joy, and contentment.

10 Gratefulness is an essential component of the life of prayer. As we grow in awareness of all that we have been given, and the rich abundance of life in God, thanksgiving breaks forth spontaneously.

"Pray earnestly even though you do not feel like praying for it is helping you even if you do not feel it doing you good, even if you see nothing, yes, even if you think you cannot pray; for in dryness and in barrenness, in sickness and in weakness, then your prayers give me great pleasure, even if you feel that they are hardly pleasing to you at all. And it is so in my sight with all your trustful prayers."[9]

LT 41, P. 100

And thanksgiving is also part of prayer. Thanksgiving is a new inward awareness, accompanied by great reverence and loving fear, when we apply ourselves with all our might to whatever action our good Lord inspires, rejoicing and giving inward thanks. And sometimes thanksgiving is so abundant that it breaks out into words and says, "Good Lord, thank you; blessed may you be!"[10]

LT 41, P. 100

11 Julian continues to develop the interrelationship between prayer and trust. The two need to be held in balance; both should be "equally abundant." As we come to know God's kindness and mercy toward us, we trust that our truest prayers spring from God's life in us. We grow in confidence and live out of our hope in God.

12 As a theologian, Julian repeatedly directs the reader to remember that God is the source of being in whom we can dwell and be at home. This is a belief that requires stamina and endurance, engaging both our will and our power to think.

13 From the cross, in the moment of his Passion, the Lord has led Julian to see three things clearly. Human beings have been created in the image and likeness of God, sustained by divine breath. Next, we have been "redeemed"—an ancient term meaning to be bought back from slavery and set free—by Jesus's death on the cross. Finally, all has been made for us and for our flourishing, kept in being as an act of love, sustaining the human family.

For this is what our Lord wants—that both our prayers and our trust should be equally abundant; for if we do not trust as much as we pray, our prayers do not fully honor our Lord and we also hinder and harm ourselves; and I believe that the reason is this: we do not truly know that our Lord is the foundation from which our prayers arise and neither do we know that this is given to us by the grace of his love; for if we knew this, it would make us confident that our Lord would give us everything we desire; for I am sure that no man asks for mercy and grace with true sincerity unless mercy and grace have already been given to him.[11]

LT 42, P. 101

He wants us to have a true knowledge that he himself is Being, and he wants our understanding to be rooted with all our might and all our will-power and all our thought in this knowledge, and on this foundation he wants us to build our home and our dwelling place.[12]

LT 42, P. 102

And by his own gracious light he wants us to understand the following things: the first is our noble and excellent creation; the second our costly and precious redemption; the third, everything which he has made beneath us to be of use to us and which he sustains out of love for us.[13]

LT 42, P. 102

14 The life of prayer is a life of yearning created in us by God. When we are stirred by that longing and loving, we turn Godward in our prayer and in our lives. Our trust deepens as we come to befriend this God who has loved us into being, sustains us at every moment, and receives us at our end.

15 Although the soul is always united to God, we seldom allow it to reflect and mirror the divine love in whose image we are created. Only persistent prayer allows us to cooperate with the Spirit in renewing the soul and aligning our wishes and desires with God's.

Lack of the bliss for which we have been ordained by nature makes us long, and true understanding and love, with sweet thoughts of our Savior, by God's grace make us trust. And our Lord watches us continually as we perform these two actions; they are what we owe him, and his goodness allows him to allot us no lesser duties.[14]

LT 42, P. 103

Prayer unites the soul to God; for though the soul, restored through grace, is always like God in nature and substance, yet because of sin on man's part, it is often in a state which is unlike God. Then prayer testifies that the desire of the soul is the desire of God, and it comforts the conscience and fits man to receive grace. And so God teaches us to pray, and to trust firmly that we shall obtain what we pray for; because he regards us with love and wishes to make us sharers in his good deed, and therefore he moves us to pray for what it pleases him to do; and for these prayers, and for the good will that he wishes us to show him, he will reward us and give us an everlasting recompense.[15]

LT 43, P. 103

16 Julian contends that God is grateful to us for our fidelity in prayer and in love. God's gratitude toward those who turn toward God's love is as infinite as that love, and as surprising. In this immense spiral of love, God's pleasure in the circulating of life, love, and light increases our own pleasure in seeking God.

17 Here Julian describes the depths of contemplative prayer. It is that moment in which we rest in God with our whole being, a moment in which we know our true home, so that all speech, all thought, and all concepts are no longer needed. This is the fruit of God's own presence and active loving within us, a joyous gift beyond price.

18 Once the soul begins to see God and glimpse the love that makes us and sustains us, our God-given hunger for divine light and love begins to increase. Reoriented through prayer, the soul hungers for the food that lasts.

And this was shown in these words, "If you pray for it."
In this statement God revealed such great pleasure and so
much delight that it seemed as if he was deeply grateful to
us for every good deed that we do—and yet it is he who
does them—and because we entreat him very strongly to
do everything that pleases him; as if he said, "Then what
could please me more than to be entreated very strongly,
truly and eagerly to do what I wish to do?" And thus
through prayer the soul is in accord with God.[16]

LT 43, P. 103

But when our courteous Lord shows himself to our soul
through his grace, we have what we long for; and then for a
time we are unaware of anything to pray for; our only aim
and our whole strength is set entirely on beholding God;
and to me this seems an exalted, imperceptible prayer; for
the whole purpose of our prayer is concentrated into the
sight and contemplation of him to whom we pray, feeling
marvelous joy, reverent fear and such great sweetness and
delight in him that at that moment we can only pray as he
moves us.[17]

LT 43, PP. 103–104

And I know very well that the more the soul sees of God,
the more it longs for him, through his grace.[18]

LT 43, P. 104

19 Initially Julian received her revelations at the point of death. Later, over the years of reflecting and praying, she came to realize that she saw infinite kindness and wisdom in Christ's speaking to her from the cross. God's kindness, wisdom, and power are a divine gift that, if we consent, will infuse the whole of our lives.

20 Notice that Julian directs us to be aware of God with our senses. The senses of taste, touch, sight, hearing, and smell are all inherently good (for they are God-given) and are consecrated in this journey of prayer. No doubt her regular participation in the Eucharist informs this passage. Her experience is of a fully incarnate Lord, known to us through our senses. Our prayer is quickened and deepened as we are led to know God's life in all places and at all times, embodied and present to us in and through our senses.

21 Julian is fond of threes, which reflects her devotion to the Trinity. In this case, she tells us that in prayer we find that truth, wisdom, and love all lead us to behold and delight in God.

Then I saw that his continual operation in all manner of things is done so kindly, so wisely and so powerfully that it surpasses all our imagining and all that we can believe and think; and then we can do no more than contemplate him, rejoicing, with a great and powerful longing to be completely united with him, resting in his dwelling, enjoying his love and delighting in his kindness.[19]

LT 43, P. 104

And we shall all be unendingly held in God, seeing him truly, feeling him fully, hearing him spiritually, smelling him delectably and swallowing him sweetly; and then we shall see God face to face, fully and familiarly; the creature that is made shall see and endlessly contemplate God, who is the Maker; for no man can see God like this and continue to live, that is to say in this mortal life, but when through his special grace God wishes to show himself here, he strengthens the created being beyond its own nature, and he apportions the showing according to his own purpose, as much as is good for it at that moment.[20]

LT 43, PP. 104–105

Truth sees God, and wisdom contemplates God, and from these two comes the third, a holy and wonderful delight in God, who is love.[21]

LT 44, P. 105

22   As we pray, God continues to open our eyes and sharpen our understanding. That is how we come to discover our capacity to behold the divine life all around us and within us. This is the life for which we are intended, and it leads us to see our neighbors and the whole world as God's own beloved.

23   Julian knows that life is always a mix of joy and pain, delight and suffering. She reminds us to be faithful in prayer, and that prayer will strengthen our trust in God that is the hallmark of faith. But Julian is also realistic about our all-too-human limitations, which make us ambivalent—she refers to this ambivalence as living in a "mixed state" throughout our lives. Too often our vision is blurred and we overlook or forget the fact that God is forever with us.

24   Faith, one of the three theological virtues along with hope and love, is a gift of the Holy Ghost. Faith is the mother of all other virtues, for the essence of faith is trust in God. While it may include trust in the teachings of the church, faith is never limited to that. Faith is alive; faith and trust are ways of being and doing. Our deepest selves are formed by trust in God's love and mercy, which grows within us, nurtured and encouraged by God's own spirit.

And in his goodness he opens the eye of our understanding
and by this we gain sight, sometimes more and sometimes
less, according to the ability that God gives us to receive it.[22]

LT 52, P. 125

But then this is our comfort: that through our faith we
know that by the power of Jesus Christ, our protector, we
never consent to it [blindness], but we are discontented
with it, and endure pain and woe, praying until the time
when he shows himself to us again. And so we remain in
this mixed state all the days of our life.[23]

LT 52, PP. 125–126

And our faith is a virtue which comes from the essence of
our nature into our sensory being through the Holy Ghost,
and in this virtue all virtues come to us, for without it no
man may receive virtue: it is no less than a right understanding with true belief and sure trust of what we cannot
see, that in our essence we are in God, and God in us.[24]

LT 54, PP.130–131

25 Faith and trust are gifts given to us from the moment of our creation, when our souls are breathed into our bodies. As God's own creatures we possess the inherent gifts that allow us to grow in trust by cooperating with the Holy Spirit. Each particular life offers its own distinctive expression of faith and trust.

26 Julian sees that each life is a part of a glorious whole. Each life, so miniscule in and of itself, is connected to the vast web of life held in being by God.

27 The oneness of love has clear implications for the ways in which we think about salvation. Julian would be surprised by some of our notions about individual salvation today, such as the question, "Have you been saved?" Following early Christian writers, she understands that it is not a question of individual salvation; we are all saved *together*. All creatures, and the cosmos itself, originate from one divine source; at our death we all return to that source. In our lives here, moreover, that love indwells all and weaves us together in ways we cannot fathom.

28 God is within us, at home, patiently and kindly awaiting our recognition. As Maker of all, God is in everything, present in all places and at all times.

Our faith comes from the natural love of our soul and from
the bright light of our reason and from the steadfast perception of God which we have when we are first made. And
when our soul is breathed into our body, at the moment
when we become sensory beings, mercy and grace immediately begin to work, taking care of us and protecting
us with pity and love; and as they do so the Holy Ghost
shapes in our faith the hope that we shall rise up again to
our essential being, into the virtue of Christ, increased and
accomplished through the Holy Ghost.[25]

LT 55, p. 131

For if I look solely at myself, I am really nothing; but as one
of mankind in general, I am, I hope, in oneness of love with
all my fellow Christian;[26] for upon this oneness depends the
life of all who shall be saved; for God is all that is good, as I
see it, and God has made all that is made, and God loves all
that he has made, and he who loves all his fellow Christians
for God's sake, loves all that is;[27] for in those who shall be
saved, all is included: that is to say, all that is made and the
Maker of all; for in man is God, and God is in everything.[28]

LT 9, p. 54

29 Julian cautions against focusing too much on the personal and the particular at the expense of broader religious insight. Although she does speak out of her own experience, she does not insist that the experience should be the same for everyone. Rather than imposing her visions on others, she asks for them to serve as a way to begin to reflect on God's gracious and generous love for all.

30 The capacity to see God in everything is a spiritual gift that brings true joy. Our desire for control eases, for we see that all is in God's hands, who is working in and through all circumstances to lead us to the same end.

31 Evil, parasitic as it is, lives off divine goodness. Yet Julian intuits that in a mysterious and loving way, God is powerful enough to use even evil to a good end. God may change evil by a loving refusal to do violence. Only God's own life ultimately thwarts evil through mercy, grace, kindness, and compassion.

And then I was answered in my reason as though by a friendly intermediary, "Take these showings generally, and consider the kindness of the Lord God as he gives them to you; for it honors God more to consider him in all things than in any particular thing." I assented, and with this I learned that it honors God more to have knowledge of everything in general than to take pleasure in any one thing in particular.[29]

LT 35, P. 89

The fullness of joy is to see God in everything; for by the same power, wisdom and love with which he made all things, our good Lord is continually leading all things to the same end and he himself shall bring this about; and when the time comes we shall see it.[30]

LT 35, P. 89

I am not saying that any evil is to be praised, but I am saying that our Lord God's willingness to endure evil is praiseworthy, and through his goodness will be recognized forever in his wonderful compassion and kindness, through the operation of mercy and grace.[31]

LT 35, P. 90

32 In beholding Jesus on the cross, Julian sees that in that Incarnation God is eternally bound to us, abiding in our lives and continually healing our wounds and binding up our brokenness. And God will choose to live with us until every last soul has been gathered into bliss.

We know through our Christian faith that God alone took
on our human nature and none but he; and further that
Christ alone performed all the works needed for our salvation, and none but he; and in just the same way he alone is
now carrying out the final task: that is to say, he is living here
with us, ruling and governing us in this life and bringing us to
his bliss. And he will do so as long as any soul that will come
to heaven is still on this earth; and to such an extent that if
there were no more than one such soul, he would be with it
alone until he had brought it up to his bliss.[32]

LT 80, P. 173

1 The soul is created to seek God, and the search will involve both suffering and trust. Nevertheless, the soul that embarks on this lifelong journey is accompanied and led by the Holy Spirit. Those who experience those moments of perceiving God's merciful and loving presence discover God's own beauty.

2 The theological virtues of faith, hope, and love guide the soul along the way. Joy wells up as the soul discovers God's presence.

3 Julian causes us to reflect on the gift of renewed life that comes to us as the soul seeks to behold the face of divine love.

4 In imagery that recalls Julian's description of God as our clothing, here she sees us enclosed within God as in a household. God is a joyous host, welcoming all to a royal feast, embracing each guest, and filling all present with grace and delight.

8 □ The Soul

And this vision instructed my understanding that it pleases God a great deal if the soul never ceases to search; for the soul can do no more than seek, suffer and trust, and souls that do this are moved by the Holy Ghost; and the splendor of having found God comes by his special grace when it is his will.[1] Seeking with faith, hope and love pleases our Lord, and finding pleases the soul and fills it with joy.[2] And thus my understanding was taught that seeking is as good as finding for the time that our soul is allowed to labor.[3]

LT 10, P. 57

And at that my understanding was lifted up into heaven where I saw our Lord as a lord in his own house who has invited all his beloved servants and friends to a solemn feast. Then I saw the Lord take no seat in his own house, but I saw him reign royally there, and fill it with joy and delight, himself gladdening and comforting his beloved friends familiarly and courteously, with a marvelous melody of endless love in his own fair, blessed face; the glorious face of the Godhead which fills heaven full of joy and bliss.[4]

LT 14, P. 62

5 Once the soul begins to perceive God's own infinite generosity and joy, its growth in the likeness of God begins. The image of God within us, which might be cloudy or indistinct, becomes clearer, and we begin to shine with the radiance of God's generosity and joy, embodied through compassionate service to others.

6 Julian's radical vision of God's presence in everything leads her to know with her whole being that each person is in God whether or not he or she is aware of it. The natural, God-given inclination of the soul is good. Our life in faith is gradual maturing into that truth, and allowing the transforming effects of God's mercy and generosity to draw us into the "measure of the full stature of Christ" (Ephesians 4:13).

7 While Julian is a mystic, she is also a realist. She knows that we often act in ways that alienate us from God and our calling to embody compassion in our daily lives. Even so, God is always on our side, offering strength and courage in the face of our failures and weakness.

8 Eternal life, the life of God, dwells within us, for God is in everything. As we face into this stunning and glorious reality, we become resilient and "pliant." The brittle behaviors of self-righteousness fall away. We come to know that love is at work in all and through all, even when that seems to be completely contrary to all appearances. Julian holds on to the fact that the Christ who spoke to her from the crucifix in those moments when she was so close to death reveals only love, kindness, mercy, and joy.

And the more the loving soul sees this generosity in God, the gladder he is to serve him all the days of his life.[5]

LT 14, P. 63

What could make me love my fellow Christians more than to see in God that he loves all who shall be saved as though they were one soul? For in every soul that shall be saved there is a godly will which never consented to sin and never shall; just as there is an animal will in our lower nature which can have no good impulses, there is a godly will in our higher nature which is so good that it can never will evil but only good; and that is why God loves us and why we do what pleases him for ever.[6]

LT 37, P. 93

Peace and love always live in us, being and working, but we do not always live in peace and love; so God wants us to pay attention to this: he is the foundation of our whole life in love, and moreover he watches over us for ever and is a powerful defense against our enemies, who attack us fiercely and furiously; and our need is the greater because we give them the opportunity when we fall.[7]

LT 39, P. 96

But our good Lord the Holy Ghost, who is eternal life dwelling in our souls, keeps us safe, and brings peace to our souls, giving them comfort through grace and harmony with God and making them pliant.[8]

LT 48, P. 110

9 Julian reiterates that there is no anger in God. Any anger we may perceive is a misperception on our part, a lack of vision.

10 When we are buffeted about by shattering events and seem to have lost our orientation in life, Julian counsels us to remember that God is the "firm ground" of our prayer. God is the ground of our souls and bodies. God's steadfast love does not change.

11 Julian reminds us that at times of distress, overcome by circumstances beyond our control, we may be thought of as "dead" by others and even by ourselves. At those times we must remember that our life is in God, to whom nothing is lost. The soul does not die.

12 God, who is one and who is infinite is with us in heaven, on earth, and in our souls.

The soul is quickly united to God when it truly finds inner peace, for in God no anger can be found.[9]

LT 49, P. 113

So God is our firm ground, and he shall be our bliss and make us as unchangeable as he is when we are there.[10]

LT 49, P. 113

And through the distress and sorrow that we ourselves fall into, the earthly judgment of men often considers us dead, but in the sight of God the soul that shall be saved was never dead, nor ever shall be.[11]

LT 50, P. 114

But he wants us to have faith that he is unfailingly with us, and in three ways. He is with us in heaven, true man in his own person drawing us upwards, and that was shown in the holy thirst, and he is with us on earth, leading us, and that was shown in the third revelation, where I saw God in an instant; and he is with us in our souls, dwelling there for ever, guiding and caring for us, and that was shown in the sixteenth revelation, as I shall describe.[12]

LT 52, P. 126

13   Our wills are good because they come from God. We have the God-given ability to choose to love God and our neighbor.

14   Julian tells us that the soul is made, but out of "nothing that is made." By this she means that the soul is of God's own life.

15   Our bodies, on the other hand, are created out of the earth. Here Julian is referring to the creation story in Genesis, whereby God formed Adam "from the dust of the ground, and breathed into his nostrils the breath of life" (2:7). We are both "slime" and soul, united together, by the hidden and loving work of God.

16   We who are created from the earth are indissolubly linked to God, whose own vitality brought forth our souls and crafted our bodies. We are the stuff of God's own life.

17   Nothing can come between our soul and God, because the soul is of God and is in God. The soul does not die, for its life is the life of God and can never be separated from God.

18   The love of God, which knows no end, which suffuses the whole cosmos and indwells each soul, protects us from all evil and preserves us in mercy. Nothing can change this. We are hidden with Christ in God's own life.

I saw and understood very clearly that in every soul that will be saved there is a godly will which never agreed to sin, nor ever shall; this will is so good that it can never intend evil, but always and constantly it intends good and does good in the sight of God.[13]

LT 53, P. 128

And thus I understood that man's soul is made of nothing, that is to say, it is made, but of nothing that is made,[14] and in this way: when God was going to make man's body, he took the slime of the earth, which is a substance mixed and gathered from all bodily things, and from this he made man's body; but for the making of man's soul he did not wish to take anything at all, he simply made it.[15] And so created nature is justly united to the Creator, who is essential uncreated nature, that is, God.[16] And that is why there neither can nor shall be anything at all between God and man's soul.[17] And in this eternal love man's soul is kept whole, as the contents of the revelations mean and show; and in this eternal love we are guided and protected by God and shall never be lost; for he wants us to know that our soul is a living creature, which, through his goodness and grace, will last in heaven for ever, loving him, thanking him, praising him. And just as we shall be eternally, so we were treasured and hidden in God, known and loved since before time began.[18]

LT 53, P. 129

19 Julian's theological anthropology, which emphasizes the essentially noble and divine nature of humanity, is based on her conviction that we can never be separated from Christ. Christ's soul is our greatest virtue and we are to become as he is.

20 Julian uses the imagery of a knot to communicate how intimately Christ is tied to God and we are tied to Christ.

21 All of the souls that will be saved are intimately tied to Christ, and this union cannot be undone.

22 Because at the deepest level, we are in Christ, and Christ is in us, Julian sees no hierarchy. She believes that the most insignificant human being is as beloved by God as Christ, for there is "no distinction" made by God.

23 Perhaps alluding to the "mutual indwelling" found in the Gospel of John, Julian says that our soul abides in God and at the same time, God abides in the soul. Both of these spiritual realities are true. We have no dwelling apart from God, while God is pleased and desires to dwell within our soul. When we embrace this reality, we discover who we truly are.

Therefore he wants us to know that the noblest thing he ever made is humankind, and its supreme essence and highest virtue is the blessed soul of Christ.[19] And furthermore he wants us to know that his precious soul was beautifully bound to him in the making with a knot which is so subtle and so strong that it is joined into God; and in this joining it is made eternally holy.[20] Furthermore, he wants us to know that all the souls which will be eternally saved in heaven are bound and united in this union and made holy in this likeness.[21]

LT 53, P. 129

And in the great and endless love which God has for all mankind, he makes no distinction in love between the blessed soul of Christ and the least soul that will be saved; for it is very easy to believe that the dwelling of the blessed soul of Christ is most high in the glorious Godhead, and truly, as I understand in what our Lord conveyed, where the blessed soul of Christ is, there is the essential being of all the souls that will be saved in Christ.[22] We ought to rejoice greatly that God dwells in our soul, and we ought to rejoice much more greatly that our soul dwells in God. Our soul is made to be God's dwelling place, and the dwelling place of the soul is God, who is not made. It shows deep understanding to see and know inwardly that God, who is our Maker, dwells in our soul; and deeper understanding to see and know that our soul, which is made, dwells in God's being; through this essential being—God—we are what we are.[23]

LT 54, P. 130

24 Our age has trouble with the idea of embodiment. We perceive the body either as an instrument to be efficiently used or, at the other end of the spectrum, as something that is imperfect, shameful, unworthy of esteem. Instead, Julian insists that God indwells our "sensory being," by which she means our physical sensing and feeling body. Julian recognizes that our senses are created by God and that they are singularly hallowed by God's choosing to indwell us, body and soul. Because they are united in one sacred whole, the God who abides in our soul abides in our body.

25 Our soul is so intimately and exquisitely united with God that we have difficulty discovering and knowing it. Oddly enough, it is easier for us to begin by desiring to deepen our relationship of love with God. Julian is confident that when we begin that process, we will eventually discover the radiant, living truth of our soul, for the soul is in God. So, if we seek God, sooner or later we will also come to know our own soul.

Thus I understand that the sensory being is grounded in nature, in mercy and in grace, and this ground enables us to receive gifts which lead us to eternal life; for I saw quite certainly that our essential being is in God, and I also saw that God is in our sensory being; for at the very point that our soul is made sensory, at that point is the city of God, ordained for him since before time began; a dwelling place to which he comes and which he will never leave, for God never leaves the soul in which he dwells blissfully for ever. And this was seen in the sixteenth showing where it says, "Jesus will never leave the position which he takes in our soul."[24]

LT 55, P. 132

And thus I saw quite certainly that it is easier for us to attain knowledge of God than to know our own soul; for our soul is so deeply grounded in God, and so eternally treasured, that we cannot attain knowledge of it until we first know God, the Maker to whom it is united. But in spite of this, I saw that for complete understanding we have to long to know our own soul wisely and truly; and for this reason we are taught to search for it where it is to be found, and that is in God.[25]

LT 56, P. 133

26 God is nearer to us than our breath, than our blood, than our thoughts and imaginings. In the words of Psalm 139:13, God "knit us together in our mother's womb," sensory being and soul both woven together. We are naturally in God and with God, and that enduring and essential grounding in God is true reality.

27 For Julian, our physical selves exist in space and time, while the soul exists eternally. God dwells in both, for the sensory aspect is united to the soul. The body is a "noble city" belonging to the Lord, in which he is "enclosed." Our soul is enclosed in Jesus. It's a double enclosure— the Lord in the body, the soul in the Lord, all peacefully resting in God.

28 As long as we do not know our true identity and fail to recognize that our soul is in God, we stumble and fall into confusion. Yet our ever-faithful God leads us and guides us in love, seeking to restore our sight that we might behold the truth of the tender love and longing God has for us.

God is nearer to us than our own soul, for he is the ground
on which our soul stands and he is the means by which
essential being and sensory being are kept together, so that
they shall never be separated; for our soul sits in God in complete rest and our soul stands in God in complete strength
and our soul is naturally rooted in God in eternal love.[26]

LT 56, P. 133

And so far as our essential being and sensory being are
concerned, they may rightly be called our soul, and that is
because they are united in God. The noble city in which our
Lord Jesus sits is our sensory being, in which he is enclosed;
and our essential being is enclosed in Jesus, with the blessed
soul of Christ sitting and resting in the Godhead.[27]

LT 56, PP. 133–134

And I saw quite certainly that we must needs be in a state
of longing and suffering until the time when we are led so
deeply into God that we really and truly know our own
soul. And indeed I saw that into these great depths our
good Lord himself leads us, in the same love with which
he made us, and in the same love with which he bought us
through mercy and grace by virtue of his blessed Passion.[28]

LT 56, P. 134

29 Following the teaching of her church about the Incarnation, Julian reflects that in Jesus's conception and birth, God's own eternal love for matter and sensory life is embodied. The Incarnation itself is a showing. From all eternity, God has loved matter. In fact, one might say that divinity and matter are wedded. Julian declares that God binds himself to humanity, body and soul, in the Virgin Mary's womb, thereby revealing the depths of divine love and yearning. In that historical moment, that point in time of conception, God's desire to become fully one with us was realized. This binding of God to humanity and all that has been made cannot be undone because it is God who has accomplished it.

30 God loves all that is made, both in general and in particular. Julian's breathtaking insight is that just as God yearns for all of humanity, so God yearns for every single person. If I assume that God's love for me does not extend to others, I have failed to grasp the truth. Julian sees and understands that God delights in each and every person, and only when our hearts and souls accept this truth does the true compassion of God move within our lives. Further, because God makes, loves, and keeps each person, and we all come from that same love, we are joined to one another as part of a vital, intricate whole.

31 Julian is asking ultimate questions of her showings, wondering what death will bring and whether we will be held by God through all our fear, dread, and suffering. Her visions assure her that Jesus, who is our friend, reveals in his suffering on the cross that we are always in God. She knows that although evil flourishes, it is never the last word. Evil may appear to triumph, in this space and time, but ultimately, because love always holds itself back from violence, it will outlast evil and receive us in joy.

These virtues and gifts are treasured up for us in Jesus
Christ; for at the same time that God bound himself to our
body in the Virgin's womb, he took on our sensory soul,
and in doing so he enclosed us all within himself and united
the sensory soul with our essential being, a union in which
he was perfect man; for Christ, having bound into himself
each man who shall be saved, is perfect man.[29]

LT 57, P. 136

It is God's will that I should feel myself as much bound to
him in love as if all that he has done had been done for me.
And in his heart every soul should think of those he loves
and is loved by in this way—that the love of God unites
us to such an extent that when we are truly aware of it, no
man can separate himself from another.[30] And so our soul
ought to think that all that God has done was done for
it; and he shows us this to make us love him and to fear
nothing but him; for he wants us to understand that all the
strength of our Enemy is committed into our Friend's hand,
and therefore the soul that knows this truly will fear none
but him that it loves; it sets all other fears among sufferings
and bodily sickness and mental apprehensions.[31]

LT 65, P. 150

32 Our soul, God's own life within us, dwells at the heart of our being. God is at the very core of our essence, making that space a microcosm of the whole world, a "glorious city."

33 Jesus is seated in the very heart of each person. Royal, handsome, and of great stature, he resides within the soul, governing in peace and love.

34 Julian believes it is impossible for Jesus to abandon our souls, for there he finds his home. Furthermore, Jesus delights in this abode of the soul, and his joy is to live to the utmost the creaturely life we have been given.

And then our Lord opened my spiritual eyes and showed me my soul in the middle of my heart. I saw the soul as large as if it were an endless world and as if it were a holy kingdom; and from the properties I saw in it I understood that it is a glorious city.[32] In the center of that city sits our Lord Jesus, God and man, a handsome person and of great stature, the highest bishop, the most imposing king, the most glorious Lord; and I saw him dressed imposingly and gloriously. He sits in the soul, in the very center, in peace and rest. And the Godhead rules and protects heaven and earth and all that is: supreme power, supreme wisdom and supreme goodness.[33]

LT 67, P. 153

It seems to me that in all eternity Jesus will never leave the position which he takes in our soul; for in us is his most familiar home and his everlasting dwelling. And in this he showed the pleasure he takes in the way man's soul is made; as well as the Father might make a creature, and as well as the Son could make a creature, so the Holy Ghost wanted man's soul to be made, and so it was done.[34]

LT 67, P. 153

1 In response to her quandary about sin and evil, Julian is given the parable of the lord and the servant. A parable is a story that may appear simple on the surface, but has layers of deeper meaning. Apparently, Julian's years of reflection and prayer have led her to think even more deeply about the problem of sin and punishment. Are human beings to be blamed for their offenses against God and one another? Is there blame in a loving God?

2 Julian sees the parable as a narrative that unfolds before her at the same time as she receives increasing insight into its meaning. Thus her reading of her visions is itself a form of *lectio divina* that she has carried out over many years. So there are two ways that Julian comes to interpret her showings—first she describes the initial impact of these images as she first saw them on her sickbed, and then she revisits, digests, and savors them, achieving insight slowly over a long period of time.

3 The two characters of the parable, the lord and the servant, are highly symbolic, as is the entire story. Julian first tells us that the lord truly loves the servant and that the servant reciprocates, rushing off in "great haste" to accomplish all that the lord desires.

9 □ Parable of the Lord and the Servant

But yet at this point I was amazed and marveled most earnestly in my soul, thinking as follows: "My good Lord, I see that you are truth itself and I know for certain that we sin grievously every day and deserve to be bitterly blamed; and I can neither give up the knowledge of this truth, nor can I see that you show us any kind of blame. How can this be?"[1]

LT 50, P. 114

And then our kind Lord answered by showing in very mysterious images a wonderful parable of a lord who has a servant, and he gave me sight to aid my understanding of both.[2]

LT 51, P. 115

The first kind of vision was this: the bodily likeness of two people, a lord and a servant, and with this God gave me spiritual understanding. The lord sits with dignity, in rest and peace: the servant stands waiting reverently in front of his lord, ready to do his will. The lord looks at his servant lovingly and kindly, and he gently sends him to a certain place to do his will. The servant does not just walk, but leaps forward and runs in great haste, in loving anxiety to do his lord's will.[3]

LT 51, P. 115

4 The servant falls into a ditch through no fault of his own. If anything, the servant is injured because he is too eager to fulfill the lord's wishes. Lying in a ditch, hurt and shocked, the servant cannot behold the lord's face. His unlucky plight is all that exists for him—the ditch, the darkness, the pain, the disorientation, the helplessness. He endures "seven great torments," which include bruising, bodily weakness, loss of reason, inability to rise, isolation, loneliness, and being in a place full of difficulties.

5 Julian sees no fault or blame in the servant. He has fallen not because he is careless or sinful, but as a result of his impetuous good will and desire to carry out his task.

And he falls immediately into a slough and is very badly hurt. And then he groans and moans and wails and writhes, but he cannot get up or help himself in any way. And in all this I saw that his greatest trouble was lack of help; for he could not turn his face to look at his loving lord, who was very close to him, and who is the source of all help; but like a man who was weak and foolish for the time being, he paid attention to his own senses, and his misery continued, and in this misery he suffered seven great torments.[4]

LT 51, P. 115

I marveled at how this servant could humbly suffer all that misery. And I watched carefully to see if I could perceive any fault in him, or if the lord would blame him at all; and in truth there was no fault to be seen, for his good will and his great longing were the only cause of his fall; and he was as willing and inwardly good as when he stood before his lord ready to do his will.[5]

LT 51, P. 116

6   The lord regards the injured servant with the eyes of mercy and kindness. There is no hint of retribution, wrath, or punishment. In fact, in this vision the lord is filled with sorrow for the servant's pain and isolation, and decides how he may help him with his presence and support. Therefore he offers not only to restore the servant to health, but to do far more to compensate him for his misery.

7   Julian sees that the servant's fall is occasion for a lavish gift on the part of the lord. Rather like the father in the parable of the prodigal son (Luke 15:11–32), the lord rejoices to honor the servant, and to offer him far more delight and joy than he had ever known.

And this is how his loving lord tenderly continued to consider him, and now in two ways. Outwardly he regarded him gently and kindly, with great sorrow and pity, and this was the first way; the second was more inward, more spiritual, and this was shown when my understanding was led into the lord. I saw him rejoicing greatly because of the honorable rest and nobility to which he would and must bring his servant through his plentiful grace. This was the second kind of showing; and now my understanding took me back to the first, while keeping both in my mind. Then this kind lord said within himself, "Look, look at my beloved servant, what injury and distress he has received in my service for love of me, yes, and all because his will was good! Is it not reasonable that I should compensate him for his terror and his dread, his hurt and his injury and all his misery? And not only this, but would it not be proper for me to give a gift that would be better for him and give him more glory than if he had never been injured? Otherwise it seems to me that I would do him no favor."[6]

LT 51, P. 116

I saw that, given his own greatness and glory, it needs must be that his dear servant whom he loved so much should be truly and blissfully rewarded for ever, more than he would have been if he had not fallen; yes, and to such an extent that his fall and the misery it caused him should be transformed into great and surpassing glory and eternal bliss.[7]

LT 51, PP. 116–117

8 As Julian watches this parable unfold, its deeper meaning is not immediately obvious. Her visions both reveal and hide. Like the parables of Jesus, the parable of the lord and the servant is mysterious, somewhat like a Zen koan, and requires that Julian sit with it at length before trying to figure it out.

9 Here Julian notes the three stages through which her own comprehension of the parable must pass. First is the literal meaning of the story as it was initially presented to her, while the second is the deeper and more inward understanding she gained after twenty more years of reflection. The third is the way in which the parable illumines not only the whole of the showings, but also her entire text.

In this mysterious parable, three aspects of the revelation
remain largely hidden;[8] yet I saw and understood that each
of the showings is full of mysteries, and so I ought now
to enumerate these three aspects and the limited progress
I have made in understanding them. The first is the early
stage of teaching which I understood from it while it was
being shown to me; the second is the inner learning which
I have come to understand from it since then; the third is
the whole revelation from beginning to end, as set out in
this book, which our Lord God in his goodness often shows
freely to the eyes of my mind. And these three are so united
in my mind that I neither can nor may separate them.[9]

LT 51, P. 117

10 Julian tells us that long after the original gift of the showings, she is told inwardly to revisit them and attend to each detail of her visions. Note that she has continued to return to that initial epiphany for years. In our age of instant feedback her humility and patience have much to teach us. She does not trust her own interpretations until they have been tested and tried; when she is told to revisit and revise her understanding of the parable, she is obedient. Steeped in the life of an anchorite, enclosed for years in silence and solitude, Julian has had to learn to distinguish among the conflicting inner voices that tend to arise in deep quiet. In the way of one who seeks wisdom, always desiring deeper instruction, Julian returns to the highly concrete details of the parable, including what clothes the lord and the servant wear, their posture and stance, what they say, and what they do.

And through these three, united as one, I have been taught how I ought to believe and trust in our Lord God: that just as he showed it out of his goodness and for his own purpose he will explain the vision to us when he so wishes. Because twenty years after the time of the showing, all but three months, I received an inner teaching, as follows: "You need to pay attention to all the properties and conditions of what you were shown in the parable, though they may seem mysterious and insignificant in your eyes." I accepted this willingly and with great eagerness, looking inwardly with great care at all the details and properties which were shown at the time of the vision, so far as my wit and understanding would serve. I began by looking at the lord and the servant, and the way the lord was sitting, and the place where he sat, and then the color of his clothing and the way it was shaped, and his outward appearance, and the nobility and goodness within; I looked at the way the servant stood and where and how, at the sort of clothing he wore, its color and shape, at his outward behavior and at his inner goodness and his readiness.[10]

LT 51, pp. 117–118

11 As she revisits the images, Julian sees clearly that the lord is God and the servant is Adam, who in his fall stands for all humanity.

12 The servant's misery comes from the fact that he is unable to carry out the commands of his lord and even to see his master clearly— Julian attributes this to a profound spiritual blindness. Thus the servant, who is Adam, cannot recognize the presence of the Divine, nor can he clearly see himself and how he appears in the eyes of his lord. Thus he is radically disoriented, suffering from "great sorrow and grievous misery."

13 The parable of the lord and the servant was given to Julian in response to her questioning about the role of sin. She has fully embraced the revelation that there is no anger in God, yet she continues to wonder what her new understanding means with regard to justice. Sin pervades human life; surely there is to be some sort of divine justice that will punish those who deserve it. The parable teaches her otherwise. From God's perspective, sin is a result of men and women's ignorance and bad choices. It is not an essential flaw in human nature, nor the sum of who we humans are. The Lord desires to heal us and restore our sight. He desires to offer us whatever means are necessary for us to call upon the divine grace for the cleansing of our sight.

The lord who sat with dignity, in rest and peace, I understood to be God. The servant who stood in front of the
lord, I understood that he represented Adam, that is to say,
that one man and his fall were shown in that vision to make
it understood how God considers any man and his fall; for
in the sight of God all men are one.[11]

LT 51, P. 118

This man's strength was broken and enfeebled; and his
understanding was numbed, for he turned away from looking at his lord. But in the sight of God his purpose remained
undiminished; for I saw our Lord commend and approve
his purpose, but the man himself was obstructed and blind
to the knowledge of this purpose, and this causes him great
sorrow and grievous misery; for neither can he clearly see
his loving lord, who is most gentle and kind to him, nor can
he see truly how he himself appears to his loving lord.[12]

LT 51, P. 118

And this was the beginning of the teaching revealed to me
at this same time, through which I might come to know
God's attitude to us in our sin. And then I saw that only
suffering blames and punishes, and our kind Lord comforts
and grieves; he always considers the soul cheerfully, loving
and longing to bring us to bliss.[13]

LT 51, P. 118

14 In the parable, the lord is not reigning from afar, but sitting humbly, "alone in the wilderness." As in the beginning of the parable, here Julian's description is extremely vivid as to clothing and facial expression—she even notices the color of his hair and eyes. This vision of divinity is a vision of a flesh-and-blood person, not a force. This is a vision of embodied love, in human guise, humbly on this earth, offering infinitely capacious refuge for all.

15 Julian confirms again that God's kindly way of being with us is full of joy, full of bliss. In contrast to many of her contemporaries, she insists that the showings reveal not a God of wrath, but one whose essence is joy and love. God may sorrow over our sins, yet the divine joy in all that God has made, and especially in the human family, is abundant and without end.

The place where our Lord sat was humble, on the barren earth, deserted, alone in the wilderness. His clothing was full and ample, as befits a lord; the cloth was as blue as azure, most sober and comely. His expression was merciful, the color of his face a comely brown with pronounced features; his eyes were black, most comely and handsome, appearing full of tender pity; and within him there was a great refuge, long and wide and all full of endless heavens.[14]

LT 51, P. 118

And his tender expression as he kept looking at his servant, especially when he fell, I thought it could melt our hearts with love and break them in two with joy. The comely expression showed a handsome mixture which was wonderful to look at: it was partly sorrow and pity, partly joy and bliss. The joy and bliss are as far beyond sorrow and pity as heaven is above earth.[15]

LT 51, P. 119

16 Julian further discerns that this servant who is Adam is also Jesus Christ, the new Adam. In Jesus, God recapitulates the whole of history. It is a new beginning, with an even more glorious end. Julian sees this servant figure in a typology like that of Paul: "Thus it is written, 'The first man, Adam, became a living being'; the last Adam became a life-giving spirit. But it is not the spiritual that is first, but the physical, and then the spiritual. The first man was from the earth, a man of dust; the second man is from heaven" (1 Corinthians 15:45–47). Out of his great mercy the lord followed his servant, Adam, even into the depths of hell.

17 Julian sees that the fullness of divinity is revealed in the Incarnation of God's life in Jesus. She also knows that God's life is ultimately hidden and mysterious. God shows himself as our "familiar," as one of our own family. At the same time, God ultimately transcends all that is, beyond our language, our thoughts, our categories, and certainly our fallibility and ignorance.

18 From the beginning of time, God has appointed the soul as a royal city, the divine place of dwelling. That desire is from God; it cannot be ultimately thwarted. In the tenderest of images, Julian declares that through this parable she sees that God chooses to dwell with us in the wilderness that is our life, the realm of human daily existence. From that point, God desires to rule gently and kindly from the throne within our earthly lives, which is a barren place, a desert.

The sorrow in the Father's pity was for the fall of Adam, his most loved creature; the joy and bliss was for his beloved Son, who is equal to the Father. The merciful gaze of his tender expression filled the whole earth and went down with Adam into hell, and this unending pity kept Adam from everlasting death.[16] And this mercy and pity remain with mankind until the time we come up into heaven. But man is blind in this life, and therefore we cannot see our Father, God, as he is. And when, out of his goodness, he wants to show himself to man, he shows himself in a familiar way, like a man; nevertheless I saw truly that we should know and believe that the Father is not a man.[17]

LT 51, P. 119

But his sitting on the barren earth in a deserted place means this: he made man's soul to be his own city and his dwelling-place, the most pleasing to him of all his works; and once man had fallen into sorrow and pain he was not fit to serve that noble purpose, and therefore our kind Father would prepare no other place for himself but sit upon the earth waiting for mankind, who is mixed with earth, until the time when, through his grace, his beloved Son had bought back his city and restored its noble beauty with his hard labor.[18]

LT 51, P. 119

19 Julian carefully observes and lists details of the servant's clothing. It is old, sweat-stained, and tattered, and it doesn't fit. It is not appropriate for the circumstances in any way, so threadbare that it seems to be on the verge of completely falling apart. What could this mean?

20 In spite of his ragged dress, the servant bears witness to his deep and continuing love for his lord. His clothing may be falling apart and ill fitting, but he is full of love. His desire is to serve this lord with great-hearted obedience, ready to fulfill the lord's request as soon as it is made known.

And yet I marveled as I considered the lord and the afore-
mentioned servant. I saw the lord sitting with dignity, and
the servant standing reverently in front of his lord; and
there is a double meaning in this servant, one without and
another within. Outwardly, he was simply dressed, as a
laborer might be who was ready to work, and he stood very
near the lord, not right in front of him, but a little to one
side, on the left. His clothing was a white tunic, unlined,
old and all spoilt, stained with the sweat of his body, tight-
fitting and short on him, only reaching about a hand's
breadth below the knee, threadbare, looking as if it would
soon be worn out—in rags and tatters. And I was very surprised about this, thinking, "Now this is unsuitable clothing, for such a well-loved servant to wear in front of such an
honorable lord."[19]

LT 51, PP. 119–120

Love was shown deep within him, and this love which he
had for the lord was just like the love which the lord had
for him. His servant's wisdom saw inwardly that there was
one thing he could do which would be to the lord's honor.
And the servant for love, with no regard for himself or for
anything that might happen to him, leapt quickly forward
and ran at his lord's command to perform his will and serve
his glory.[20]

LT 51, P. 120

21 The servant is a gardener; his vocation and labor directly engage the soil. He sweats and digs, plants and tends. This servant, who is the new Adam and our true humanity, is also the symbol of our right relationship with the earth and with all that is created. The servant tends the earth in love; his daily labor brings forth plentiful food, thereby honoring the lord while serving him with great joy. In John's Gospel, when Jesus appears to Mary Magdalene outside the empty tomb, she mistakes him for a gardener (John 20:15). This imagery of gardening also evokes Eden, a garden that has been restored and made fruitful beyond measure, for the God who makes it also loves and keeps it through the care of his servant.

22 The origin of all is God; earth itself comes forth from the "wonderful depths of endless love." There is no other source, and there is no other end. The servant's role is one of grateful cooperation, gladly offered. When the servant is given the aid offered by his lord, then he is able to fulfill this vocation of increasing the joy of the lord. Without this collaboration, barren wilderness takes over.

I watched, wondering what kind of labor it could be that the servant should do. And then I understood that he would do the greatest labor and the hardest toil of all—he would be a gardener, digging and ditching, toiling and sweating, and turning the earth upside down, and delving deeply and watering the plants at the right time. And this would continue to be his work, and he would make fresh water flow, and noble and plentiful fruits spring up, which he would bring before the lord and serve him as he wished. And he should never turn back until he had prepared this food all ready as he knew it pleased the lord, and then he should take this food, with the drink as part of it, and carry it very reverently to the lord. And all this time the lord would sit in the same place, waiting for the servant whom he had sent out.[21]

LT 51, PP. 120–121

And yet I wondered where the servant came from; for I saw that the lord has within himself eternal life and every kind of goodness, except for the treasure which was in the earth—and that had its origin in the lord in wonderful depths of endless love—but it was not entirely to his glory until this servant had prepared it nobly in this way, and brought it to him, into his own presence; and without the lord there was nothing but a wilderness.[22]

LT 51, P. 121

23 In explicating the parable of the lord and the servant, Julian also seeks to clarify her own language. She explains that the figure of the servant has more than one meaning—at the same time he is humanity and divinity, both Adam and the Son of God, the second person of the Trinity.

24 In her straightforward, vernacular way, Julian restates the profound insights received from the earliest councils of the church. The Son, as second person of the Trinity, is fully God; the Son, as Jesus Christ, is fully human. That is why Julian can say, "When Adam fell, God's son fell." She is pressing the insight articulated by early church theologians: "What is not assumed is not saved."[1] To put it colloquially, in Jesus, God is with us all the way. Because of this essential unity of God and humanity, we are called forth from every hell, every valley of the shadow of death. We are called toward life, and God gives us the means to answer "yes" with our whole being.

25 Julian, like Paul, sees that all humanity, all reality, is in Christ. She discerns that every person is already in Christ, for God is the one from whom all life springs. But because Christ is the head of the body and we are the limbs, we cannot see the future or know what God knows of our true end and purpose. We must simply trust in the Holy Spirit, which sustains, guides, and loves each person.

In the servant is comprehended the second Person of the Trinity, and in the servant is comprehended Adam, that is to say, all men. And therefore when I say "the Son," it means the Godhead, which is equal with the Father, and when I say "the servant," it means Christ's Humanity, which is truly Adam.[23] The servant's nearness represents the Son, and his standing on the left side represents Adam. The lord is the Father, God; the servant is the Son, Christ Jesus. The Holy Ghost is the equal love which is in both of them. When Adam fell, God's son fell; because of the true union made in heaven, God's son could not leave Adam, for by Adam I understand all men. Adam fell from life to death into the valley of this wretched world, and after that into hell. God's son fell with Adam into the valley of the Virgin's womb (and she was the fairest daughter of Adam), in order to free Adam from guilt in heaven and in earth; and with his great power he fetched him out of hell.[24]

LT 51, p. 121

Therefore what was conveyed was in respect of the Manhood of Christ; for all mankind who shall be saved by Christ's precious Incarnation and blessed Passion, all are Christ's manhood. He is the head and we are his limbs; and these limbs do not know the day and the time when every passing grief and sorrow will come to an end, and everlasting joy and bliss will be accomplished, the day and time which all the company of heaven longs to see.[25]

LT 51, p. 122

26 Julian's perspective, conferred on her by these revelations, leads her to see that Jesus is fully identified and fully united to all humans. The initiative is divine, not human. We do not bring about this union by any efforts of our own. It already exists.

27 Julian sees the Divine-human relationship in rich and varied ways, and through multiple metaphors. God is not only a father to us, but also a mother, a spouse, a bridegroom, a brother, a savior. All of these dimensions of relationship are revealed in and through Jesus, who extravagantly and faithfully loves the humanity that is his own being.

28 Julian knows fully that in this life we will always experience both sorrow and joy, heartache and delight. Because we are human, it is always a mixture of "weal and woe." Yet we may trust, as she saw in the parable of the lord and the servant, that our true royal destiny is to be where Christ is—in other words, eternally at the heart of God.

For Jesus is all who shall be saved and all who shall be saved
are Jesus; and all through God's love, along with the obedience, humility and patience, and other virtues which per-
tain to us.[26]

LT 51, PP. 122–123

And so I saw that God rejoices that he is our father, and
God rejoices that he is our mother, and God rejoices that
he is our true spouse, and our soul is his much-loved bride.
And Christ rejoices that he is our brother, and Jesus rejoices
that he is our savior. These are five great joys, as I understand it, in which he wishes us to rejoice, praising him,
thanking him, loving him, endlessly blessing him.[27]

LT 52, P. 125

All people who shall be saved, while we are in this world,
have in us a marvelous mixture of both weal and woe. We
have in us our risen Lord Jesus; we have in us the misery of
the harm of Adam's falling and dying.[28]

LT 52, P. 125

1 In Jesus Christ, God has united divinity to all humanity. What is accomplished through divine love and mercy cannot be undone. Jesus's earthly mother, the Virgin Mary, is therefore spiritually our mother. We humans, ever knitted to divinity through this infinite and tenacious love, are born from Mary spiritually as Jesus is born from her physically.

2 Mary's source and being are from God who is revealed in Jesus. He is her spiritual mother. Jesus, the Savior, is also our mother. We are eternally born from Jesus, and we are eternally enclosed in him. Julian reminds us throughout the text that the second person of the Trinity is the Word made flesh, Jesus. Remember that Julian, as both mystic and theologian, speaks of the Trinity as a single, unified reality known as Father, Son, and Holy Ghost. So when she writes of Jesus as the second person of the Trinity, whom she identifies as both Wisdom and Mother, she is speaking of God.

3 Just as a mother steadily teaches, holds, feeds, and tends her child, so God is with us. When we are attentive to God's teaching and guidance, we continue to learn how to behave as God's own children.

4 The second person of the Trinity, who is known in Jesus, is also our mother, with regard to both our soul and our physicality. Both aspects of human life come from God's wisdom, the second person of the Trinity and our mother.

10 □ The Motherhood of God

Thus our Lady is our mother in whom we are all enclosed and we are born from her in Christ; for she who is mother of our Savior is mother of all who will be saved in our Savior.[1] And our Savior is our true mother in whom we are eternally born and by whom we shall always be enclosed.[2] This was shown abundantly, fully and sweetly, and it is spoken of in the first showing where he says that we are all enclosed in him and he is enclosed in us; and it is spoken of in the sixteenth showing, where it says that he sits in our soul; for it is his pleasure to reign blissfully in our understanding, and to sit restfully in our soul and to dwell endlessly in our soul, working us all into himself; and in this working he wants us to help him, giving him all our attention, learning what he teaches, keeping his laws, desiring that everything he does should be done, faithfully trusting in him; for I saw truly that our essential being is in God.[3]

LT 57, P. 136

I saw that as the second Person is mother of our essential being, so that same well-loved Person has become mother of our sensory being; for God makes us double, as essential and sensory beings.[4]

LT 58, P. 138

5   In Jesus, God shows us that humanity and divinity are one. Both our physical and our spiritual natures are united because they come from this mother. We can never be apart from this love, this mother, "in whom our parts are kept unparted."

6   Here Julian explicitly calls God our mother, and she means this not only as metaphor, but as spiritual and eternal reality. She sees that God is the matrix in which all exists, and that God's own being encloses everything that is. This seems to suggest a divine womb, an enfolding space in which we are ever nurtured and birthed anew. If God is our mother, it follows that we are created from that life, and that our deepest and truest human expression is found in remembering that we are made in the image of self-offering love. Julian's way of seeing is rich and complex, for God's paternity is not eclipsed, but fully complemented. All of God's revealed relational identities hold true at the same time.

The second Person of the Trinity is our mother in nature and in our essential creation, in whom we are grounded and rooted, and he is our mother in mercy in taking on our sensory being. And so our Mother, in whom our parts are kept unparted, works in us in various ways; for in our Mother, Christ, we profit and grow, and in mercy he reforms and restores us, and through the power of his Passion and his death and rising again, he unites us to our essential being. This is how our Mother mercifully acts to all his children who are submissive and obedient to him.[5]

LT 58, P. 138

Thus Jesus Christ who does good for evil is our true mother; we have our being from him where the ground of motherhood begins, with all the sweet protection of love which follows eternally. God is our mother as truly as he is our father; and he showed this in everything, and especially in the sweet words where he says, "It is I," that is to say, "It is I: the power and goodness of fatherhood. It is I: the wisdom of motherhood. It is I: the light and the grace which all blessed love. It is I: the Trinity. It is I: the unity. I am the sovereign goodness of all manner of things. It is I that makes you love. It is I that makes you long. It is I: the eternal fulfillment of all true desires."[6]

LT 59, P. 139

7 │ Following the scholastic theology of Thomas Aquinas, Julian reminds the reader that in giving us our human nature, God also restores that nature and makes it glorious through grace. Her particular wisdom is that it is God's motherhood that bequeaths these gifts to us—both a nature that is of God's own being and the grace that leads that nature to flourish and become more like God. We discover God's maternity as we truly behold our nature and the gift of grace, revealed to Julian as she beheld Jesus's dying on the cross.

8 │ Julian understands in threes, for trinitarian theology is imprinted deeply on her way of knowing. She speaks of God's motherhood being known to us in our creation, in grace, and in God's working in us for love.

9 │ God, our mother, breathed new life into our humanity through the conception of Jesus. In that period of gestation God knit us together, and knit us both from divine life and to divine life. Just as Jesus was hidden within his mother Mary's womb until he was born, so our true identity is hidden and enclosed within the Virgin's womb. This way of speaking points to those perennial questions of "Who am I?" and "How shall I be in this world?" Julian recognizes the truth of God's own maternity; for her that recognition is a release from the captivity of mistaken identity and an assurance of God's ongoing, gentle work within our depths.

And so Jesus is our true mother by nature, at our first creation, and he is our true mother in grace by taking on our created nature. All the fair work and all the sweet, kind service of beloved motherhood is made proper to the second Person; for in him this godly will is kept safe and whole everlastingly, both in nature and in grace, out of his very own goodness.[7]

LT 59, P. 140

I understood three ways of seeing motherhood in God: the first is that he is the ground of our natural creation, the second is the taking on of our nature (and there the motherhood of grace begins), the third is the motherhood of works, and in this there is, by the same grace, an enlargement of length and breadth and of height and deepness without end, and all is his own love.[8]

LT 59, P. 140

Our natural Mother, our gracious Mother (for he wanted to become our mother completely in every way), undertook to begin his work very humbly and very gently in the Virgin's womb.[9]

LT 60, P. 141

10 In Julian's day, when a woman prepared to give birth, she also prepared for the possibility of death. Childbed fever, a postpartum infection, led to the deaths of many women in Julian's day. So life and death were intimately intertwined, particularly in the act of birthing. Julian brings that knowledge to bear upon her vision of Jesus's dying on the cross. His death gives life, just as the birth of a child was known to be accompanied by the death of the mother in so many instances. Jesus, fully God, bears us into eternal life and love through the birth pangs of his dying. His Passion is a kind of labor and delivery; his death pangs are contractions. She sees his suffering as the anguish of a woman in the throes of labor, and like a mother he is willing to endure the pain with love so that we may be born into bliss.

11 Just as a mother nurses her child, feeding the baby with milk from her own body, so Jesus feeds us with himself. Julian intentionally links the bread and wine of Communion, sacraments of Christ's body and blood, to his desire to nourish us with his own divine life.

The mother's service is the closest, the most helpful and the most sure, for it is the most faithful. No one ever might, nor could, nor has performed this service fully but he alone. We know that our mothers only bring us into the world to suffer and die, but our true mother, Jesus, he who is all love, bears us into joy and eternal life; blessed may he be! So he sustains us within himself in love and was in labor for the full time until he suffered the sharpest pangs and the most grievous sufferings that ever were or shall be, and at the last he died. And when it was finished and he had born us into bliss, even this could not fully satisfy his marvelous love; and that he showed in these high surpassing words of love, "If I could suffer more, I would suffer more."[10]

LT 60, P. 141

He could not die any more, but he would not stop working. So next he had to feed us, for a mother's dear love has made him our debtor. The mother can give her child her milk to suck, but our dear mother Jesus can feed us with himself, and he does so most generously and most tenderly with the holy sacrament which is the precious food of life itself.[11]

LT 60, P. 141

12 In the account of the crucifixion from the Gospel of John, we are told that after Jesus died, a soldier "pierced his side with a spear, and at once blood and water came out" (19:34). Julian links that blood and water to the amniotic fluid and blood of childbirth. Just as she began with the image of a hazelnut in her hand, showing the relationship between all that exists and the infinite nature of God, so in this passage she sees the side of Christ to be so capacious that it easily houses all that is. We, and the whole cosmos, dwell within the side of this Jesus, our mother. As we are shown his pierced side, we see the wounds of divine love, eternally longing for us and ever gifting us with maternal nurture and sustenance.

13 This passage, which may reveal something of Julian's own life as a mother, speaks wisely of formation. Just as a mother will allow her child to make mistakes while growing and maturing, so too with God, our mother. Just as she knows that sometimes, in order for character to be formed surely and steadily, a child needs to learn to accept consequences, so too with God. As both our father and our mother, God offers us the gracious gift of a love that knows who we really are, and how our lives will be kindly and surely transformed when we allow grace to work within us. Julian assumes that we will grow and mature in the life of prayer and faith. Because so much of that growth occurs as we live with our failures, we will come to know our need of this divine love. She understands this to be a lifelong process, one in which God is constantly guiding us as a parent, while also allowing us the freedom of love.

The mother can lay the child tenderly to her breast, but our tender mother Jesus, he can familiarly lead us into his blessed breast through his sweet open side, and show within part of the Godhead and the joys of heaven, with spiritual certainty of endless bliss; and that was shown in the tenth revelation, giving the same understanding in the sweet words where he says, "Look how I love you," looking into his side and rejoicing.[12]

LT 60, PP. 141–142

This fair, lovely word "mother," it is so sweet and so tender in itself that it cannot truly be said of any but of him, and of her who is the true mother of him and of everyone. To the nature of motherhood belong tender love, wisdom and knowledge, and it is good, for although the birth of our body is only low, humble and modest compared with the birth of our soul, yet it is he who does it in the beings by whom it is done. The kind, loving mother who knows and recognizes the need of her child, she watches over it most tenderly, as the nature and condition of motherhood demands. And as it grows in age her actions change.[13]

LT 60, P. 142

14 As our mother, God wisely allows us to fall, for only then will we come to know our innate need of God's mercy and strength. "We need to fall." We arrive at the radical awareness that a life lived autonomously, as if we were self-made, is a lie. We discover again and again our built-in need for one another and our essential need for God. God's love for us is as persistent as a loving mother's, and nothing we do can alter that.

If we fall, he quickly raises us by calling us tenderly and touching us with grace. And when we have been strengthened like this by his dear actions, then we choose him willingly, through his precious grace, we choose to serve him and to love him forever and ever. And after this he allows some of us to fall harder and more painfully than we ever did before, or so it seems to us. And those of us who are not very wise think that all our earlier effort has gone for nothing. But it is not so; for we need to fall, and we need to be aware of it; for if we did not fall, we should not know how weak and wretched we are of ourselves, nor should we know our Maker's marvelous love so fully; for in heaven we shall see truly and everlastingly that we have sinned grievously in this life, and we shall see that in spite of this his love for us remained unharmed, and we were never less valuable to him. And by experiencing this failure, we shall gain a great and marvelous knowledge of love in God for all eternity; for that love which cannot and will not be broken by sin is strong and marvelous.[14]

LT 61, P. 143

15 Here Jesus is compared to a "kind nurse," which connotes both a mother whose milk gives life to her child, and a healer of the sick. Julian refers specifically to the hands of the Savior, hands eternally marked by the nails of the crucifixion. She has beheld these hands and knows that the wounds bear witness to the love that holds us and will not let us go.

16 Julian gathers up her insights and offers this concise summary: God, our mother and father, is the One from whom we come, the One in whom we live and move and have our being, and the One to whom we will return. Because God is love, this divine nature expressed so kindly as both mother and father is our deepest identity and our home.

17 Traditionally, the church itself has been seen as a maternal presence through which the Savior offers nurture and renewal, as well as discipline and instruction. In the motherly love of the church, the soul finds what is necessary for true life. Julian seeks to reconcile her experiences with the received tradition of the medieval church. Sometimes she seems to be at variance with church doctrine; nevertheless, she takes pains to stress her fidelity to what she has learned from the church, even when there is great tension between what she has been taught and what these revelations have led her to understand.

The blessed wounds of our Savior are open and rejoice to heal us; the sweet gracious hands of our Mother are ready and carefully surround us; for in all this he does the work of a kind nurse who has nothing to do but occupy herself with the salvation of her child. His task is to save us, and it is his glory to do so, and it is his wish that we know it; for he wants us to love him tenderly, and trust him humbly and strongly. And he showed this in these gracious words, "I hold you quite safely."[15]

LT 61, P. 144

God in his essence is kindly nature; that is to say, the goodness that is kind and natural is God. He is the ground, he is the substance, he is kind nature itself and he is true father and true mother of nature.[16]

LT 62, P. 145

Here we can see that we do not need to search far and wide to know various kinds of nature, but seek them in Holy Church, in our mother's breast; that is to say, in our own soul, where our Lord lives. And there we shall find everything; find it now in faith and in understanding, and later find it truly in himself and brightly in bliss.[17]

LT 62, P. 145

[18] Jesus is our mother in our making, our keeping, our loving. His maternal relationship with us is truly one of being birthed into this earthly life and through rebirth and transformation in Jesus's Passion and death on the cross. Love brings life out of death. Jesus's love brings forth life infinitely more glad and glorious, for his motherly desire is that we be nurtured, sustained, and formed by that love. Julian leads us to see that we are to be childlike in our trust of the divine, full of wonder and joy. Here she seems to be inspired by Jesus's words about children: "Let the little children come to me, and do not stop them; for it is to such as these that the kingdom of heaven belongs" (Matthew 19:14). Julian directs us to remember our essential dependence upon God's grace and mercy, and to recognize Jesus as the mother who births us anew.

So our life is grounded in our true mother, Jesus, in his own foreseeing wisdom since before time began, with the great power of the Father, and the great and supreme goodness of the Holy Ghost. And in taking on our human nature he gave us life, in his blessed death on the cross he gave us birth into life everlasting; and from that time, and now, and for ever until Judgment Day, he feeds and fosters us, just as the great and supreme kind of nature of motherhood and the natural need of childhood demand. To the eyes of our soul, our heavenly Mother is good and tender; to the eyes of our heavenly Mother the children of grace are precious and lovely, with humility and gentleness and all the fair virtues which belong to children by nature; for naturally the child does not despair of the mother's love; naturally the child does not set itself up presumptuously; naturally the child loves the mother and each one loves the other; these are the fair virtues, with all others that are like them, with which our heavenly Mother is honored and pleased.[18]

LT 63, P. 147

19 Julian reminds us that we never outgrow our need of God our mother. In this life, we will always be upheld and nursed by our mother's own care and wisdom. Upon our deaths we will awaken to the truth of Julian's saying, "All shall be well," for we will be reborn into the fullness of God—father, mother, friend, brother, spouse, and home.

And I understood that in this life no one grows beyond
childhood, in feebleness and inadequacy of body and mind,
until the time when our gracious Mother has brought us up
into our Father's bliss. And then we shall really understand
what he means in these sweet words where he says, "All
shall be well, and you shall see for yourself that all manner
of things shall be well." And then the bliss of our motherhood in Christ will begin again in the joys of our God; a
new beginning which will last without end, always beginning again.[19]

LT 63, P. 147

1 | Jesus makes it clear to Julian that her visions are no figment of her imagination, "no delirium." These are true insights, and his intent is that she know that his Passion has defeated evil (the Fiend) and that all of us may live in the confidence that we will not be overcome. We may trust fully in all that she has received and written for her readers.

11 □ All Shall Be Well

He said very lovingly, "Know well now that what you saw today was no delirium; accept and believe it, hold to it and comfort yourself with it and trust to it, and you shall not be overcome." These last words were said to prove to me with full assurance that it is our Lord Jesus who showed me everything. And just as in the first phrase which our good Lord revealed, referring to his blessed Passion—"By this is the Fiend overcome"—in just the same way he said his last phrase with very great certainty, referring to all of us, "You shall not be overcome."[1]

LT 68, P. 155

2 Julian hands on what she has received from the Lord. He tells her that she will not be overcome, and after mulling this over, she adds that he did not say life would be without pain and struggle. Though she may know torments, her confidence is in the God who speaks through Jesus on the cross.

3 After some twenty years of going over the visions, writing them down, allowing them to be held gently in prayer and informed by Scripture, Julian trusts that they are true. She believes that they are God-given, and that all shall be well.

4 The love-longing that characterizes the divine relationship with humanity goes both ways. God longs and thirsts for us as we long and thirst for God. As we come to know that truth, we begin to live with the confidence that "all shall be well."

And all this teaching of true comfort applies without exception to all my fellow Christians, as I said before, and it is God's will that it should be so. And these words, "You shall not be overcome," were said very loudly and clearly for security and comfort against all the tribulations that may come. He did not say, "You shall not be tormented, you shall not be troubled, you shall not be grieved," but he said, "You shall not be overcome." God wants us to pay attention to these words and wants our trust always to be sure and strong, in weal and woe; for he loves and is pleased with us, and so he wishes us to love and be pleased with him and put great trust in him; and all shall be well.[2]

LT 68, P. 155

I believe that he who showed it is our Savior, and that what he showed is the true faith. And therefore I believe and rejoice in it; and I am bound to do so by what he said himself in the words which follow next: "Hold to it and comfort yourself with it and trust to it." Thus I am bound by my faith to believe it.[3]

LT 70, P. 157

Glad and cheerful and sweet is the blessed, loving face with which our Lord looks at our souls; for he is constantly in love-longing towards us while we live, and he wants our souls to look gladly on him so as to give him his reward.[4]

LT 71, P. 158

5 | The revelations of divine love were given to Julian so that she might tell her fellow Christians the truth of this love. God gave Julian these visions in order to write them down, to pray with them for years, and then to offer her wisdom and insight to others. All of this is intended for her evenchristen, who are God's "heavenly treasure on earth."

This book was begun by God's gift and his grace, but it seems to me that it is not yet completed. With God's inspiration let us all pray to him for charity, thanking, trusting and rejoicing; for this is how our good Lord wants us to pray to him, as I understood from all that he conveyed, and from the sweet words where he says very cheeringly, "I am the foundation of your prayers"; for I truly saw and understood in what our Lord conveyed that he showed this because he wants to have it better known than it is. Through this knowledge he will give us grace to love and cling to him; for he feels such great love for his heavenly treasure on earth that he wants to give us clearer and more comforting sight of heavenly joy as he draws our hearts to him, because of the sorrow and darkness which we are in.[5]

LT 86, P. 179

6 In this famous passage, Julian confesses her own quandary. Fifteen years after receiving the revelations, she boldly asked about the meaning of what she had seen. The answer, in one word, was "love." Love from all time and forever. Love indwelling all that is. Love that is our truest self and the life of our soul. Love that will vanquish evil by refusing to answer violence with violence. Love that is real, true, and beautiful. Love that is our beginning. Love that is our end.

And from the time that this was shown, I often longed to know what our Lord meant. And fifteen years and more later my spiritual understanding received an answer, which was this: "Do you want to know what your Lord meant? Know well that love was what he meant. Who showed you this? Love. What did he show? Love. Why did he show it to you? For love. Hold fast to this and you will know and understand more of the same; but you will never understand or know from it anything else for all eternity." This is how I was taught that our Lord's meaning was love. And I saw quite certainly in this and in everything that God loved us before he made us; and his love has never diminished and never shall. And all his works were done in this love; and in this love he has made everything for our profit; and in this love our life is everlasting. We had our beginning when we were made; but the love in which he made us was in him since before time began; and in this love we have our beginning. And all this shall be seen in God without end, which may Jesus grant us. Amen.[6]

LT 86, P. 179

7 | In her final words to us, Julian offers a warning. She pleads that we not merely pick and choose from her writings, and is clearly uneasy about the text falling into the wrong hands—those who will not read it with faith and trust. And lastly, she gives thanks for the God who has so gifted her, and has given her the wisdom and the patience to hand on what she has received.

I pray to almighty God that this book come only into the hands of those who want to love him faithfully, and to those who are willing to submit themselves to the faith of Holy Church and obey the sound understanding and teaching of men of virtuous life, grave years and profound learning; for this revelation is deep theology and great wisdom, so it must not remain with anyone who is thrall to sin and the Devil. And beware that you do not take one thing according to your taste and fancy and leave another, for that is what heretics do. But take everything together and truly understand that everything is in accordance with holy Scripture and grounded in it, and Jesus our true love, light and truth will show this wisdom concerning himself to all pure souls who ask for it humbly and perseveringly. And you to whom this book may come, thank our Savior Jesu Christ earnestly and heartily for making these showings and revelations of his endless love, mercy and goodness for you and to you, to be your and our safe guide and conduct to everlasting bliss; which may Jesus grant us. Amen.[7]

LT 86, P. 180

Notes ☐

Introduction

1. *Julian of Norwich: Revelations of Divine Love*, trans. Elizabeth Spearing (New York: Penguin Books, 1998), 99. All subsequent references to this text appear in parentheses.

2. T. S. Eliot, "The Dry Salvages," *The Complete Poems and Plays, 1909–1950* (New York: Harcourt, Brace and World Publishing, 1971), 133.

3. Sheila Upjohn, *In Search of Julian of Norwich* (London: Darton, Longman and Todd, 1989), 2.

4. Fr. John-Julian, OJN, *The Complete Julian of Norwich* (Brewster, MA: Paraclete Press, 2011), 21–27.

5. Kenneth Leech and Benedicta Ward, SLG, *Julian Reconsidered* (Oxford, England: SLG Press, 1992), 22–25.

6. Margery Kempe, *The Book of Margery Kempe,* trans. Barry Windeatt (London: Penguin Classics, 2000), 12.

7. Jeannette S. Zissel, "The Hazelnut in Julian of Norwich's *Showings*," in *Urban Space in the Middle Ages and the Early Modern Age*, ed. Albrecht Classen (Boston: De Gruyter Press, 2009), 333.

8. Roberta C. Bondi, "Teaching Julian of Norwich to Seminarians" (Lecture, Society of Christian Spirituality, San Antonio TX, Fall 2004).

9. ———, "Acquainted with Death," *The Christian Century* (Sept. 22–29, 1999): 906.

10. Elizabeth Petroff, *Medieval Women's Visionary Literature* (New York: Oxford University Press, 1986), 5–6.

11. Ibid., 6.

Chapter 3

1. Augustine of Hippo, *Confessions*, trans. and ed, R. S. Pine-Coffin (New York: Penguin Books, 1961), 21.

Chapter 9

1. Gregory of Nazianzus, *Gregory of Nazianzus: Collected Writings*. Fig Classic Series of Early Church Texts (No Place: Fig-Books, 2012), Kindle edition.

Suggestions for Further Reading ☐

Middle English Text

Crampton, Georgia Ronan, ed. *The Shewings of Julian of Norwich.* Kalamazoo, MI: Western Michigan University, 1994.

Translations of *Revelations of Divine Love*

Colledge, Edmund, and James Walsh, trans. and ed. *Julian of Norwich: Showings.* New York: Paulist Press, 1978.

John-Julian, Fr., OJN, trans. and ed. *The Complete Julian of Norwich.* Brewster, MA: Paraclete Press, 2011.

Spearing, Elizabeth, trans. *Julian of Norwich: Revelations of Divine Love.* New York: Penguin Books, 1998.

About Julian of Norwich

Baker, Denise Nowakowski. *Julian of Norwich's Showings: From Vision to Book.* Princeton, NJ: Princeton University Press, 1994.

Bondi, Roberta C. *Julian of Norwich.* Nashville, TN: Abingdon Press, 2007.

———. "Teaching Julian of Norwich to Seminarians." Lecture presented at Society of Christian Spirituality, San Antonio, TX, Fall 2004.

Frykholm, Amy. *Julian of Norwich: A Contemplative Biography.* Brewster, MA: Paraclete Press, 2010.

Jantzen, Grace M. *Julian of Norwich: Mystic and Theologian.* New York: Paulist Press, 1988.

Lanzetta, Beverly J. *Radical Wisdom: A Feminist Mystical Theology.* Minneapolis, MN: Fortress Press, 2005.

Leech, Kenneth, and Benedicta Ward. *Julian Reconsidered.* Oxford, UK: SLG Press, 1992.

Llewelyn, Robert. *All Shall Be Well: The Spirituality of Julian of Norwich for Today.* New York: Paulist Press, 1982.

McGinn, Bernard. "Julian of Norwich: 'Love is oure lords mening.'" In *The Varieties of Vernacular Mysticism, 1350–1550.* New York: Crossroad, 2012.

Nuth, Joan. *Wisdom's Daughter: The Theology of Julian of Norwich*. New York: Crossroad, 1991.

Turner, Denys. *Julian of Norwich, Theologian*. New Haven, CT: Yale University Press, 2011.

Upjohn, Sheila. *In Search of Julian of Norwich*. London: Darton, Longman, and Todd, 1989.

Zissel, Jeannette S. "The Hazelnut of Julian of Norwich's *Showings*." In *Urban Space in the Middle Ages and the Early Modern Age*. Edited by Albrecht Classen. Boston: DeGruyter Press, 2009.

Other Sources

Eliot, T. S. "The Dry Salvages." In *The Complete Poems and Plays, 1909–1950*. New York: Harcourt, Brace and World Publishing, 1971.

Kempe, Margery. *The Book of Margery Kempe*. Translated by Barry Windeatt. London: Penguin Classics, 2000.

Petroff, Elizabeth. *Medieval Women's Visionary Literature*. New York: Oxford University Press, 1986.

Spirituality

The Passionate Jesus: What We Can Learn from Jesus about Love, Fear, Grief, Joy and Living Authentically   *By The Rev. Peter Wallace*
Reveals Jesus as a passionate figure who was involved, present, connected, honest and direct with others and encourages you to build personal authenticity in every area of your own life.   6 x 9, 208 pp, Quality PB, 978-1-59473-393-2   **$18.99**

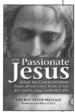

Gathering at God's Table: The Meaning of Mission in the Feast of Faith
By Katharine Jefferts Schori
A profound reminder of our role in the larger frame of God's dream for a restored and reconciled world.   6 x 9, 256 pp, HC, 978-1-59473-316-1   **$21.99**

The Heartbeat of God: Finding the Sacred in the Middle of Everything
By Katharine Jefferts Schori; Foreword by Joan Chittister, OSB
Explores our connections to other people, to other nations and with the environment through the lens of faith.   6 x 9, 240 pp, HC, 978-1-59473-292-8   **$21.99**

A Dangerous Dozen: Twelve Christians Who Threatened the Status Quo but Taught Us to Live Like Jesus
By the Rev. Canon C. K. Robertson, PhD; Foreword by Archbishop Desmond Tutu
Profiles twelve visionary men and women who challenged society and showed the world a different way of living.   6 x 9, 208 pp, Quality PB, 978-1-59473-298-0   **$16.99**

Decision Making & Spiritual Discernment: The Sacred Art of Finding Your Way   *By Nancy L. Bieber*
Presents three essential aspects of Spirit-led decision making: willingness, attentiveness and responsiveness.   5½ x 8½, 208 pp, Quality PB, 978-1-59473-289-8   **$16.99**

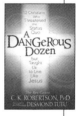

Laugh Your Way to Grace: Reclaiming the Spiritual Power of Humor
By Rev. Susan Sparks   A powerful, humorous case for laughter as a spiritual, healing path.   6 x 9, 176 pp, Quality PB, 978-1-59473-280-5   **$16.99**

Claiming Earth as Common Ground: The Ecological Crisis through the Lens of Faith   *By Andrea Cohen-Kiener; Foreword by Rev. Sally Bingham*
Inspires us to fulfill our sacred imperative to care for God's creation.
6 x 9, 192 pp, Quality PB, 978-1-59473-261-4   **$16.99**

Creating a Spiritual Retirement: A Guide to the Unseen Possibilities in Our Lives   *By Molly Srode*
Invites you to examine your spiritual life and explore ways of making it more meaningful.   6 x 9, 208 pp, b/w photos, Quality PB, 978-1-59473-050-4   **$14.99**

Creative Aging: Rethinking Retirement and Non-Retirement in a Changing World   *By Marjory Zoet Bankson*
Explores issues you need to address as you move into this period of life.
6 x 9, 160 pp, Quality PB, 978-1-59473-281-2   **$16.99**

Keeping Spiritual Balance as We Grow Older: More than 65 Creative Ways to Use Purpose, Prayer, and the Power of Spirit to Build a Meaningful Retirement   *By Molly and Bernie Srode*
Brimming with ideas to add purpose and spirit in the building of your meaningful retirement.   8 x 8, 224 pp, Quality PB, 978-1-59473-042-9   **$16.99**

Or phone, fax, mail or e-mail to: SKYLIGHT PATHS Publishing
Sunset Farm Offices, Route 4 • P.O. Box 237 • Woodstock, Vermont 05091
Tel: (802) 457-4000 • Fax: (802) 457-4004 • www.skylightpaths.com
Credit card orders: (800) 962-4544 (8:30AM–5:30PM EST Monday–Friday)
Generous discounts on quantity orders. SATISFACTION GUARANTEED. Prices subject to change.

About SKYLIGHT PATHS Publishing

SkyLight Paths Publishing is creating a place where people of different spiritual traditions come together for challenge and inspiration, a place where we can help each other understand the mystery that lies at the heart of our existence.

Through spirituality, our religious beliefs are increasingly becoming a part of our lives—rather than *apart* from our lives. While many of us may be more interested than ever in spiritual growth, we may be less firmly planted in traditional religion. Yet, we do want to deepen our relationship to the sacred, to learn from our own as well as from other faith traditions, and to practice in new ways.

SkyLight Paths sees both believers and seekers as a community that increasingly transcends traditional boundaries of religion and denomination—people wanting to learn from each other, *walking together, finding the way.*

For your information and convenience, at the back of this book we have provided a list of other SkyLight Paths books you might find interesting and useful. They cover the following subjects:

Buddhism / Zen	Global Spiritual	Monasticism
Catholicism	Perspectives	Mysticism
Children's Books	Gnosticism	Poetry
Christianity	Hinduism /	Prayer
Comparative	Vedanta	Religious Etiquette
Religion	Inspiration	Retirement
Current Events	Islam / Sufism	Spiritual Biography
Earth-Based	Judaism	Spiritual Direction
Spirituality	Kabbalah	Spirituality
Enneagram	Meditation	Women's Interest
	Midrash Fiction	Worship

Or phone, fax, mail or e-mail to: SKYLIGHT PATHS Publishing
Sunset Farm Offices, Route 4 • P.O. Box 237 • Woodstock, Vermont 05091
Tel: (802) 457-4000 • Fax: (802) 457-4004 • www.skylightpaths.com
Credit card orders: (800) 962-4544 (8:30AM–5:30PM EST Monday–Friday)
Generous discounts on quantity orders. SATISFACTION GUARANTEED. Prices subject to change.

For more information about each book, visit our website at www.skylightpaths.com